Virternity:
The quest for a virtual eternity.

A treatise on the aims and goals of
the Virternity Project.

David Evans Bailey

First published in Great Britain by VR Academic Publishing 2017

Author's Affiliated Websites

https://www.researchgate.net/profile/David_Bailey11

Cover Illustration by David Evans Bailey.

(Use of Public Domain image from NASA and NSSDC)

Contents

CONTENTS   4

ABOUT THE AUTHOR   8

FORWARD   10

INTRODUCTION   1

SUMMARY OF CHAPTERS   5

CHAPTER ONE   17

VIRTERNITY; PROJECT VIRTUAL ETERNITY, AN EXPLORATION INTO THE POSSIBILITY OF A VIRTUAL LIFE.   17

CHAPTER TWO   34

VIRTERNITY; THE GOAL OF SETTING UP A VIRTUAL/DIGITAL CURRENCY - CRYPTOCURRENCY.   34

CHAPTER THREE   51

VIRTERNITY; DISTRIBUTED EXCHANGE NETWORK: THE MARKET WITHOUT BORDERS   51

CHAPTER FOUR   69

VIRTERNITY; DEPOSIT-REFUND SYSTEM   69

CHAPTER FIVE   89

VIRTERNITY: IRIS SCAN ACCESS FOR SECURE ACCESS   89

CHAPTER SIX   104

VIRTERNITY: CONNECTION OF AUGMENTED AND VIRTUAL REALITIES. EMERGENCE OF THE SHAREABLE COMPOUND REALITY = VIRTERNITY FULLY-FEATURED SPACE   104

CHAPTER SEVEN 116

VIRTERNITY: THE VIRTUAL OFFICE 116

CHAPTER EIGHT 129

VIRTERNITY: TRANSFER AND STORAGE OF HUMAN MEMORY INTO THE VIRTERNITY ENVIRONMENT AND SHARED MEMORY (AND EXPERIENCE) EXPERIMENTING 129

CHAPTER NINE 142

VIRTERNITY: FORECAST SYSTEM BASED ON NEURAL NETWORK AND BLOCKCHAIN VIRTERNITY CONNECTIONS 142

CHAPTER TEN 152

VIRTERNITY: EXPERIMENTS WITH A DEEP IMMERSION INTO THE VIRTERNITY SPACE (LONG-TERM EXISTENCE ONLY IN THE VIRTUAL PART OF THE VIRTERNITY SPACE) 152

CHAPTER ELEVEN 164

VIRTERNITY: COPYING THE HUMAN CONSCIOUSNESS AND MEMORY TO THE VIRTERNITY SPACE (EXPERIMENTS WITH DIGITAL COPIES OF REAL PERSONS) 164

CHAPTER TWELVE 177

VIRTERNITY: ELABORATION OF LEGAL, PSYCHOLOGICAL AND FINANCIAL ISSUES OF THE EXISTENCE OF VIRTUAL PERSONS 177

CHAPTER THIRTEEN 189

VIRTERNITY: UNLINKABLE PAYMENTS (UNTRACEABLE TRANSACTIONS) IMPLEMENTATION 189

CHAPTER FOURTEEN 200

VIRTERNITY: COMMUNICATION CHANNELS DEVELOPMENT 200

CHAPTER FIFTEEN 210

VIRTERNITY: UNIVERSAL SECURE STORAGE: RESEARCH, INVENTIONS, PIECES OF ART, ETC.   210

CHAPTER SIXTEEN   222

VIRTERNITY: INTRODUCTION OF THE FIELD "TEMPORARY DATA" TO THE VIRTERNITY BLOCKCHAIN AND COMBINING EXISTING BLOCKCHAIN DATABASES INTO AN INTEGRATED 3D BLOCKCHAIN   222

CHAPTER SEVENTEEN   233

VIRTERNITY: START-OVER OF THE VIRTERNITY SPACE WORLDWIDE NETWORK. VIRTERNITY WILL BECOME EVERYDAY PRACTICE OF WORK AND LEISURE IN THE DEVELOPED COUNTRIES   233

CHAPTER EIGHTEEN   247

VIRTERNITY: VIRTUAL REALITY GAMES IN THE VIRTERNITY BLOCKCHAIN SPACE   247

CHAPTER NINETEEN   259

VIRTERNITY: FIRST SUCCESSFUL TRANSITION OF THE PERSONS INTO THE VIRTERNITY SPACE (AS SUI JURIS INDIVIDUALS WITH SOCIAL RESPONSIBILITY, WORK, SOCIAL CONTACTS, ETC.) TRANSITIONS OF PERSONS INTO THE VIRTUAL PART OF THE VIRTERNITY SPACE BECOMES EVERYDAY PRACTICE. IMMORTALITY IN VIRTERNITY AVAILABLE IN PRACTICE FOR ALL.   259

CHAPTER TWENTY   271

VIRTERNITY: HUMANITY EXISTING SIMULTANEOUSLY IN THE BOTH PHYSICAL AND VIRTUAL REALITY   271

EPILOGUE   284

FULL LIST OF REFERENCES   286

About the Author

David Evans Bailey spent his early youth in Africa. His father and mother were atypical expats who freely mixed with the community at large, regardless of race, creed or colour. He gained a liberal political foundation from his father and a love of books and literature from his well-read family. He had a long career as an IT Professional from programmer to project manager culminating with working in the City of London for over sixteen years. Following a diversion from IT fueled by major changes in his personal life, he had a spell running his own building business and then spent some years as a secondary school teacher. David feels he was always searching for his real drive and inspiration and has also always had a healthy interest in the arts. A photographer from the age of eleven this became a lifelong passion. Combining this with his IT background he became fascinated in creating digital art pieces from his photographs. This inspired him to undertake a Master's degree in Digital Media Art at the

University of Brighton from which he graduated in 2014. He moved the Auckland with his second wife in 2015 and is currently researching a Doctorate investigating the creation of Art using immersive Virtual Reality at Auckland University of Technology. After many years of searching, David believes he has finally found his métier with an academic life of research and personal art practice.

Forward

by

David Evans Bailey

I was approached by the Virternity project to write an academically based treatise based on the aims of their proposal. Their intention was to try to add more substance to their claims and ideas. I accepted the commission because apart from the fact that my current line of research is rooted in the medium of VR, I believe that VR will become a major part of our everyday lives in the future. When I studied for my MA at the University of Brighton, I wrote a thesis entitled *Hyperreality: The merging of the physical and digital worlds* (2014). One of my key conclusions in this thesis was that new virtual technologies which seem set to bind us ever closer to the digital world should be researched and studied further. It behoves us to become ever more conscious of the impact that these will have upon us in the future. With this in mind, I welcomed the opportunity to examine one such enterprise in more depth and delve into the detail that surrounds such an undertaking. It encompasses many fascinating fields including financial, technological, scientific, legal and philosophical. To create a new virtual world is not necessarily a singular idea but coupled with the immersive nature of VR, it is something that will inevitably make changes to everyday lives should it come to pass. This treatise was written to a fairly tight timescale and brief and is not intended to be an exhaustive analysis of the topics presented. Any one of the many matters raised by Virternity could, in fact, take months of work to investigate to the fullest extent. The motivation is rather to show whether it's been done, or even thought about, and whether it is or might be achievable in the future. Is there any sound basis for the statements, claims and desires that Virternity has for its new virtual world? Some of the goals that Virternity has mooted are impossible to prove at this time and have never been done before, but nevertheless, there are those who are researching those fields too. For the Virternity project, there are many challenges along the road ahead to the fulfillment of their ambitious quest. Whilst I cannot say if they are ready for those challenges, I can at least tease out a little of what those challenges are and what they face if they are to ultimately succeed. That, in essence, is the objective of this book, to present with a research bias, the opportunities that the Virternity project has before it. Whether they achieve the immortality they wish for will be up to them.

Introduction

The Virternity project is an idea which has apparently been conceived by a consortium of individuals from many disciplines and in multiple locations. This is perhaps an apt metaphor for the idea of the project itself wherein the ultimate creation of a virtual universe will contain a multitude of people both real, virtual or a mixture of both. Such fictional accounts as *Ready Player One* (Cline, 2011) have proposed the existence of a virtual space which is inhabited by the majority of the denizens of Earth, who continue their physical existence whilst spending most of their time in a digital world called *OASIS*. Aside from fiction such worlds as *Second Life* already exist and are populated by those who desire just that, a life outside the physical. Although in truth *Second Life* is prone to many of the same trials and tribulations of the real world. *Second Life* and its counterparts are more like an addendum to daily living for most and for some it might be also an extension to their normal existence. However, none of these current models of virtual worlds bills themselves as a passage to an entirely new form of existence. Virternity is, in that sense, something new. Its aims are far reaching in terms of what it proposes to offer to humanity.

There appear to be two main project development paths to Virternity. The first aims to create a virtual immersive and semi-immersive world with which people could engage. However, the framework of this new world that the Virternity project conceives go far beyond an MMORPG (Massively multiplayer online role-playing game) such as *Second Life*. The Virternity project states a clear intention to develop a virtual existence that could one day supersede the physical needs of humanity. It proposes that humans themselves may ultimately somehow be able to upload themselves into digital versions and freed from their mortal bodies live an entirely simulated computer existence in virtual space. As much as this idea may appear at first glance to inhabit the realms of science fiction there are certainly some professionals in the field of neuroscience for example who believe that this can become a scientific fact. Far from dismissing out of hand these claims to a potential future for humanity, the ideas that Virternity has need to be seriously examined in the context of what is currently possible and what might be potentially possible in the future.

There are many unknown factors at this point but nevertheless, the aims can be considered within the context of current research and contemporary thinking. Even if one excludes the extremities of their stated goals there is nevertheless a potential that people will, in the future, inhabit two worlds; the physical world that we currently know and the digital world that Virternity intends to create. In the minds of those participating between these two boundaries, the two worlds may well end up merging into one, a digital and physical dichotomy. I like to define it this way; a mergence of the digital and the physical. Mergence being a word which to me best describes this conjoining of the two universes, almost like a duality of existence. The second development path is one of a more practical nature in that it concerns the fiscal elements of such a virtual existence in the form of a virtual currency and other accompanying services such as deposit and exchange systems. These types of products and systems are already in existence outside of the Virternity project and therefore it cannot be doubted that they are also achievable for the Virternity project. For these endeavours, it is more a question of the risks and challenges that they pose. The issues surrounding these products and ideas are discussed along with the technological factors involved such as blockchain. Other technical aims such as iris scanning technology for secure access and the use of blockchain for copyright and storage of non-financial information and things are also part of this second path. It might be said that the second path supports the first and is perhaps essential to its success. Seen as a whole, the Virternity project is an encompassing idea, its aims and goals are by no means small in intention or in scope. What is or is not achievable may not be answered in this book but certainly, this is an attempt to address the challenges that lie ahead with reference to current developments and similar endeavours that are already in existence. What the reader may elicit from this book is the potential of the ideas that the Virternity project has expressed and that much of what is proposed is certainly possible or may be in the future.

Summary of Chapters

Chapter One briefly discusses the fundamental assertions and goal for the Virternity project in terms of the prospect of eternal life in the digital realm. Philosophical viewpoints on the question of consciousness are examined against the practical potential for mind uploading. The purpose of the chapter is not to engage a deep philosophical dissertation about the ontology of man but rather to set the scene and to note that there are widely differing views from which the feasibility of the ultimate aims of the Virternity project could be argued.

Chapter Two discusses one of the cornerstones and inception points for the Virternity project, the establishment of a virtual currency. The purpose of this chapter is to delineate the potential advantages and drawbacks regarding the use of a virtual currency as it relates to the Virternity project. It concludes with a brief examination in regard to the feasibility of this aspect of the Virternity project's aims and elements, noting matters which may need to be accounted for in the creation and operation of a virtual currency system.

Chapter Three discusses further the proposal of the Virternity project to establish a virtual currency exchange. It looks at some of the technological definitions and concepts involved and the feasibility of this with due reference to authorities and contemporary thinking on the topic from experts in the field.

Chapter Four discusses the proposal of the Virternity project to establish a deposit refund system for their virtual currency. It looks at the reasons for this and its feasibility again with due reference to authorities and contemporary thinking on the topic from experts in the field.

Chapter Five discusses the proposal of the Virternity project to use iris scan technology to enable secure access to the Virternity systems and assets. Current developments and the technology itself are examined as well as future potentials of this technology. The technology itself is not in its infancy and has reached a high level of sophistication. The drawbacks and potential threats to this kind of security system are also examined.

Chapter Six discusses the proposal of the Virternity project to mix augmented and immersive technologies and the resulting realities into a compound shared reality. The progress of these technologies to date are examined together with future prospects and what the feasibility is for this ultimate goal being realised. The technological foundation and the progress in this part of the field ultimately dictate what Virternity can or cannot achieve in the virtual realm. Thus, this is an important chapter in the exploration of the project as a whole.

Chapter Seven discusses the proposal of the Virternity project to provide virtual offices for those who wish to work at remote locations or even set up businesses that run in the Virternity world. Virtual offices are by no means a new idea and this chapter sets out to examine not only the feasibility of this way of working but also the desirability of it and the beneficial or otherwise effects upon productive working.

Chapter Eight discusses the proposal of the Virternity project to implement the digitised memories of people that are generated by sensor devices used in immersive, compound or mixed realities and share or 'relive' those experiences whilst in the Virternity world. The Virternity project moots this as an opportunity for personal gain without the associated risk. The possible methods of doing this are explored in this Chapter and also in Chapter Eleven.

Chapter Nine discusses the proposal of the Virternity project to enable and augment forecasting and prediction using the Virternity space. Virternity conjectures that using Neural networks and blockchain technology will allow precise analysis of future events and such things are tracking the state of a person's health and future prospects.

Chapter Ten discusses the proposal of the Virternity project to implement experiments which will see volunteers living solely through the medium of mixed reality via Virternity space. The participants are intended to live isolated from their physical existence and contact their friends and family solely through immersive and semi-immersive VR. The stated aim of these experiments is to enable Virternity developers to obtain data which could lead to the digitisation of human consciousness.

Chapter Eleven discusses the proposal of the Virternity project to engage in serious experiments that will lead to the emergence in the virtual space of 'digital copies' or what the project terms as 'people-originals'. The project designers intend that the experiments will make it possible to protect the original people from harm at this early stage. The intention is to continue the experiments until a person can be fully transferred into the Virternity space.

Chapter Twelve discusses the proposal of the Virternity project regarding legal measures that might be required within the virtual space of Virternity. Virternity also envisages that new business and social services will be available to seniors and that new issues will be raised and new solutions required: ranging from petty offences merged into the digital reality and ending with psychological and philosophical implications of new features and abilities, new experiences and ways of life. It may then be within the realm of possibility for individuals who have already spent a considerable time in Virternity space to move entirely into the virtual world.

Chapter Thirteen discusses the proposal of the Virternity project regarding the idea of making blockchain transactions untraceable in the Virternity space. Virternity asserts that some users may prefer not to leave information about their private life in the digital space and that the project should respect privacy and individual freedoms. They imply that they will provide a new feature allows a user to make payments with untraceable origins around the world.

Chapter Fourteen discusses the proposal of the Virternity project regarding the idea of reducing the speed of blockchain messaging. The Virternity team claims to have found the key to virtually instant messaging. They assert that this will introduce to the world of digital communication the main blockchain advantages - the authenticity, integrity and reliability of information. The claims will be examined in as far as possible against known data.

Chapter Fifteen discusses the proposal of the Virternity project regarding the idea of enabling a secure storage facility for valuable works. Virternity plans that they will provide a secure copyright database which will be immediately available dispensing with delays and costly registration. The right of authorship will thus be proven from the very moment of work is uploaded to Virternity storage. Virternity also contemplates that the preservation of research results, invention, pieces of artistic culture for mankind, and additionally essential science can be shared. In essence, Virternity envisages an openly published register of ownership and intellectual property rights. The Virternity project intends to provide a protected space that also allows access to materials by consent of the authors and originators.

Chapter Sixteen discusses the proposal of the Virternity project with regard to making a temporary blockchain space where information can be deleted automatically after a set period which would be user selectable with the option to turn it into permanent data prior to this. Additionally, the Virternity project asserts that they are open to all blockchain databases who want to join the project and combine the existing blockchain databases into a single super-base or a large prototype of the new digital universe.

Chapter Seventeen discusses the proposal of the Virternity project regarding their ideas that successful experiments with the advanced technologies of the future will make it possible to transfer and store all data from different information sources into the sole worldwide blockchain. They assert that all the most important parts of material reality will be digitised and repeated in the virtuality and that compound (mixed) reality devices will provide a permanent, wide exchange of information between the two realities in real time. They contend that there will be a shift towards a parallel implementation in the virtual space and that perhaps everyday things like apartments and houses, cars, furniture, restaurants, medical consultations, fashion will one day exist primarily in the virtual reality. They propose that fewer resources will be needed to sustain economic growth and mass consumption. They hypothesise that Earth will gradually be digitised (and expanded) so that prominent sights of interest will be available from the comfort of the virtuality. The net result they say is that there will be less demand for the Earth's resources since enjoyment will be transferred to a virtual life.

Chapter Eighteen discusses further the proposal of the Virternity project regarding their ideas that their virtual reality space will certainly create a space for all kinds of games. These are envisaged to be set in many different eras and contain also such experiences as visiting the Titanic, walking on the moon, flying through space will be available. People will be able to transform into fantastic forms of life, expanding the range of available experiences. They contend that the experiences will be so 'real' that the experiences would be the equivalent of having encountered them in the physical world but without the risk of harm that might entail.

Chapter Nineteen discusses the proposal of the Virternity project regarding the transition of persons into the Virternity world. Virternity asserts that for these people there will be no technological or psychological barrier for a complete transition from one world to another. They speculate that a growing number of people will make a decision to permanently move to the virtual reality where they will benefit from the adaptation to not being prone to the effects of a physical existence any longer. They envisage a smooth transfer developing the virtual component of their personality in such a way that the transition will simply be a continuation of their existence. Thus, they hope to answer the question of human immortality and that the physical body is a stepping stone to assuming a virtual digital existence. Virternity hopes to provide the solution to 'death' and the quest for eternal life. An almost reverse vector may occur where physical avatars would be controlled by virtual humans to experience the physical sensations of the planet.

Chapter Twenty discusses the proposal of the Virternity project regarding the idea of real and virtual people (people solely in virtual reality) communicating in the Virternity space. With a plethora of virtual experts thus created it is envisaged that this can be passed on through generations and that artists of all disciplines can continue to be productive in virtual space. Virtual people could also control mechanisms in conditions that could be dangerous for ordinary people. Time travel will be effected by the ability to return to past events and memories with the ability to view them internally or externally to the event. Actual decision modelling could be made to alter the course of events or even to revisit and relive past events with a different outcome. Their expectation is that this existence will lead to new philosophical questions and paths of thinking. Although they envisage a positive and green field world of opportunity unfettered by the restrictions of the physical earth, they assert that they don't expect a paradise on virtual Earth. They anticipate new economic, political and social challenges of the new society and they expect there to be people and programs engaged in law enforcement, investigation and other such activities. They even anticipate that there may be a new form of unspecified death but that the main angst of the present-day life: physical death (as well as old age, infirmity and illnesses) and depletion of resources (poverty, wars and fierce competition as well) will become irrelevant.

CHAPTER ONE

Virternity; Project Virtual Eternity, an exploration into the possibility of a virtual life.

David Evans Bailey

This chapter discusses the fundamental assertions and goal for the Virternity project in terms of the prospect of eternal life in the digital realm. Relevant philosophical viewpoints on the question of consciousness are examined against the practical potential for mind uploading. Much has been written and speculated about the potential of life in the virtual world. From the novel, *Ready Player One* (Cline, 2011) to the iconic film *The Matrix* (Wachowski & Wachowski, 1999) the idea of humanity subsuming themselves in some way within a virtually created 'reality' has been fictionalised and one might even say sensationalised. Cline puts forward an ultimately dystopic vision of a VR world where the physical world becomes almost a service industry for human participation in VR. *The Matrix* itself proposes a self-fulfilling machine that offers a parasitic existence from humans who it uses as its energy cells. In fact, *The Matrix* is loosely based upon the work of contemporary Philosopher Jean Baudrillard who writing in *Simulacra and Simulation* (1981) said this *"By crossing into a space whose curvature is no longer that of the real, nor that of truth, the era of simulation is inaugurated by a liquidation of all referentials - worse: with their artificial resurrection in the systems of signs, a material more malleable than meaning, in that it lends itself to all systems of equivalences, to all binary oppositions, to all combinatory algebra. It is no longer a question of imitation, nor duplication, nor even parody. It is a question of substituting the signs of the real for the real, that is to say of an operation of deterring every real process via its operational double, a programmatic, metastable, perfectly descriptive machine that offers all the signs of the real and shortcircuits all its vicissitudes."* (Baudrillard, 1981, p. 2). Baudrillard thus points out that in his view the future would remove the physical references to what perhaps was currently thought of as the 'real world' and create an entirely separate set of simulations in the virtual world. He goes further in explaining that it is not just the idea of replacing the physical world with the virtual but that where the 'real' can be changed and altered without reference to what it once represented. It is a somewhat bleak outlook where the virtual is taken as the 'real' world and it almost even supersedes it or overrides it. The danger he feels lies in an idea that the virtual world is perhaps like a digital sleight of hand which replaces concepts of truth and other ideas that we can reference with a new digital truth and one which may, in fact, be far from the actual truth itself. This further quote by Baudrillard is echoed in the context of the film *The Matrix* where he states *"Today abstraction is no longer that of the map, the double, the mirror, or the concept. Simulation is no longer that of a territory, a referential being, or a substance. It is the generation by models of a real without origin or reality: a hyperreal. The territory no longer precedes the map, nor does it survive it. It is nevertheless the map that precedes the territory - precession of simulacra - that engenders the territory, and if one must return to the fable, today it is the territory whose shreds slowly rot across the extent of the map. It is the real, and not the map, whose vestiges persist here and there in the deserts that are no longer those of the Empire, but ours. The desert of the real itself."* (Baudrillard, 1981, p. 2). Here Baudrillard is talking of how one usually makes a map of a piece of territory and that map is the reference to places and things within the physical world. However, in the new digital age, he implies that the map comes before the territory and in fact produces perhaps a new territory. When a real map decays it leaves the territory that it represents behind it. Almost in reverse, the digital map leaves vestiges of the original physical territory on which it might be based. This is Baudrillard's assertion; that the digital world is the focus of life and the real world has become or has been deserted. This quite dystopian outlook of virtual reality is a common idea where humanity abandons the 'real' world in favour of the digital. In *The Matrix*, the character Morpheus after explaining what the matrix is to the central hero Neo, utters the immortal phrase *"Welcome to the desert of the real"* (Wachowski & Wachowski, 1999) in an echo of Baudrillard's, some might say prophetic, words. Well before the internet and when the very first personal computers were in evidence Baudrillard predicted a world of increasing simulation, with the advent of VR it could be argued that his predictions are fast becoming actual. However, whether in fact, his view that the digital will subsume or even override the physical world is far from clear at this time. There is much speculation on this point and fiction naturally has risen to the occasion to exploit this dichotomy. Even in the early 1900's in *The Machine Stops* (Forster, n.d.) the novelist E.M. Forster wrote of a world completely run by a virtual machine which performs all duties for humans who are isolated in hexagonal chambers and talk to each other only via television like globes. In his version of an impending apocalyptic scenario, the overarching machine ultimately comes to a juddering halt with the ensuing demise of most of the humans who are held in its thrall. In many of these types of fictional accounts, there is usually some element of deception or subterfuge that plays a part in distorting this future vision by duping humans into an existence which ends up out of their control. Then, like most stories of computer controlled worlds, the humans rebel in some form and the simulations are broken or irrevocably changed.

However, what if instead one could build a virtual world with effective open borders, in a consensual and cooperative way? Perhaps the element of 'conspiracy' inherent in these types of predictions may be mitigated. The Virternity project proposes a more benign and positive outlook to the future of humanity's adventure into the virtual realm and the increasing mergence with the digital world. There is perhaps a sense of inevitability about the move towards a future where humans span both the physical and digital world. I also speculated about this same topic in my Master's thesis *Hyperreality: The merging of the physical and digital worlds* (Bailey, 2014). The thesis explored the burgeoning relationship between these two worlds and whether humanity is indeed moving closer to this merged reality until it becomes inextricably part of it. The conclusion that I came to at the end of the dissertation was that we do appear to be moving in that direction of unity with the digital world but that it is our responsibility to ensure that we all become arbiters of our new future. We cannot leave it to corporations and governments to ultimately take charge of the direction which this *digital mergence* takes. (Bailey, 2014). One entrant into this new digital arena is the Virternity project. The project bills itself as the builder of a new virtual world where those within it can indeed, as I suggested, be the arbiters of their own virtual fate and retain some control over its destiny. The creation of the Virternity world involves the idea of openness where ultimate control is not vested in any one organisation, individual or even group of individuals. This chapter introduces and discusses the overriding vision of the Virternity project, discrete parts of the project itself are discussed in more detail in further chapters.

One of the cornerstones of the Virternity concept is that of 'Eternal Life' lived in a virtual world. The idea is put forward that a person will live forever in digital form or as the Virternity vision also terms it the 'digitisation of the human cerebration'. To answer this primary goal might ultimately entail an investigation into what a human actually is, what does the mind consist of and what is human consciousness. The philosophical argument for the existence of duality of spirit or mind and matter is one that has occupied philosophers for centuries and there are indeed many that could be drawn upon from Plato or Aristotle onwards to thinkers such as Descartes or Deleuze. Contemporary and influential philosopher Henri Bergson is one of the more eminent thinkers in arguing the case regarding consciousness. I have chosen to focus particularly on his thoughts since they expose quite clearly the dichotomy that is at the heart of the ultimate aims of Virternity and its intentions for humanity. Bergson opens his own enquiry in *Matter and Memory* (Bergson, Jacobson, & Dingle, 1965) with this statement *"This book affirms the reality of spirit and the reality of matter, and tries to determine the relation of one to the other by the study of a definite example, that of memory. It is then frankly dualistic."* (Bergson, et al., 1965, p. 9). Bergson lays out his argument from the first sentence for a consciousness that is not necessarily part of material structure. From the beginning of his book, he indicates that he intends to argue the case for the duality of man, that man and thus consciousness consists of more than just the physicality of structure. Speaking of the brain itself Bergson's view is that *"In our opinion, then, the brain is no more than a kind of central telephonic exchange:*

its office is to allow communication or delay it" and that the nervous system is *"in no sense an apparatus which may serve to fabricate, or even to prepare, representations."* (Bergson, et al., 1965, p. 30-31). He shows by this very statement that he believes the brain to simply be a mechanism for transporting communication around the body. He does not imbue the brain with any apparatus by which to manufacture what he terms 'representations' and what we might imagine to be the pictures and other information that make up and inhabit the mind. To support his argument against the brain being an apparatus of conscious thought as opposed to what he asserts is a conduit he focuses on perception and by also drawing upon Leibniz's *Monadology*. Leibniz says this *"we are obliged to admit that perception and that which depends on it cannot be explained mechanically, that is, by means of shapes and motions. And if we suppose that there were a machine whose structure makes it think, feel, and have perception, we could imagine it increased in size while keeping the same proportions, so that one could enter it as one does with a mill. If we were then to go around inside it, we would see only parts pushing one another, and never anything which would explain a perception.*" (Leibniz, & Strickland, 2014, p. 17). Leibniz alludes to the idea that perception cannot be simply explained as if it were parts of a machine and that there must be more to its explanation than pure mechanics. In the same vein and using perception as his exemplar, Bergson argues that the brain itself cannot process the results of perceptions and that there must be something additional that accomplishes this feat. He argues in this way against the structure of the brain itself as being the entirety of the human condition for life. If you take his arguments to their logical conclusion, then the brain itself could not be held to be the suppository of the entirety of what defines human consciousness.

Whether or not the transfer of consciousness to a digital realm can be achieved is therefore philosophically a matter for debate but at the same time, it is also the subject of current and future experimentation. Prominent in this field, Neuroscientist Kenneth Hayworth argues that the technology for uploading the mind and preserving it in digital form will be possible in the future. In an article for Skeptic Magazine, he states *"Any discussion about mind uploading must be about what can reasonably be assumed possible in the distant future, not what is achievable today. I am certainly not arguing uploading will be easy, or that it will occur within the next few decades; but I will argue it is a technically achievable, potentially desirable, long-term goal."* (Hayworth, 2016, p. 15). Basing this upon his own knowledge and experience in the field examining structure and the working of the nervous system his conclusion is very different to that of philosophers such as Bergson. His assertion is that it certainly would be possible in the future to upload the mind to computer. In the same article, he discusses ACT-R ("Adaptive Control of Thought—Rational" a cognitive architecture mainly developed by John Robert Anderson at Carnegie Mellon University) as being relevant in creating models of the human mind *"perhaps the most complete cognitive-level architecture of the human mind today is ACT-R which has served as a basis for hundreds of publications across dozens of labs. There are ACT-R models of problem solving, attention, language, etc. These models perform on the same experimental tasks that human subject do and make testable predictions, on the fine scale of reaction times,* learning rates, fMRI activation patterns, etc." (Hayworth, 2016, p. 16). What he refers to is an attempt to simulate the cognitive and perceptual functions of the human mind by computer. The architecture and programming have, as he notes, been used to many experiments and simulations of the human mind in digital form. Based upon the success of these and model, his implication is that the way a human mind works is possible to recreate on a computational level. However, it is fair to say that simulation and consciousness may not be arguably the same thing. Thus, it is a matter for debate, but to support his argument and in conclusion, he notes *"I have presented evidence supporting the idea that human mind uploading is a technically achievable goal, albeit one that may take centuries to realise. And I have presented evidence that a potentially inexpensive and reliable preservation technique (ASC) that could... allow everyone alive today to reach that future mind uploading technology."* (Hayworth, 2016, p. 20). Essentially Hayworth asserts that uploading a mind is perfectly within the realms of possibility including all the memories and algorithmic decision processes involved in an individual's choices. His premise is based on the idea that if one can create the mind in a computer then the problem is simply how to transfer the data from an actual mind to the computer. This mind upload is not within the current realm of technology although small experiments have been done and Hayworth proposes one method as to how it could be done. It is not too remarkable to find that not everyone agrees with Hayworth's view. For example, software expert and sceptic Peter Kassan concludes in his own article for the same magazine *"The notion of uploading your own brain to computer is, if not science fiction, then certainly science fantasy based on a misunderstanding both of the overwhelming complexity (and our near-total ignorance) of the brain, and of what computer models are and what they can (and cannot) do. But even if all the insurmountable obstacles were miraculously overcome, the resulting computer – even if it was a faithful and convincing imitation of you – would not be conscious. And certainly would not be you."* (Kassan, 2016, p. 25). Kassan thus denies the possibilities that Hayworth proposes as being feasible. He indicates that no matter how sophisticated the programming and algorithms could be that in his view you cannot recreate conscious human being. He argues that you can imitate or even simulate but this would not be a conscious entity. To counter this type of viewpoint, Hayworth premises his version of consciousness upon the following assumptions from his paper *Electron Imaging Technology for Whole Brain Neural Circuit Mapping* in which he asserts that *"The most fundamental assumption on which this thesis depends is that the human mind and its conscious experiences are purely a computational phenomenon. We are broadly similar to an intelligent robot. Our body is analogous to the robot's mechanical body. Our brain is analogous to the robot's computer hardware including the physical hard drives which contain its control software. Our mind is analogous to the computational processes that result by the running of this control software on the robot. Our first-person conscious experiences are analogous to the particular stream of tokened data structures that the robot uses to model its own perceptions, goals, and actions as part of its self-model (used as a higher-order guide for reasoning about and planning its future behaviors)... Although in principle there may be some deep flaw in this analogy between a human and a mechanical robot, it is an analogy that rests at the core of all of our research in cognitive science, neuroscience, and even biology itself."* (Hayworth, 2012, pp. 89-90). To Hayworth, the human is almost reducible to electronic circuitry and artificial intelligence can be modelled upon the workings of the human decision-making processes just as if it was a computer program albeit far more complex than programming languages today. He thus likens humans as analogous to robots and his premise is that based on this view that the ability to copy and duplicate the contents of the brain into a computer would produce a conscious human being. If this was found to be absolutely the case, then what he sees as the potential to upload a mind is then a matter for technological accomplishment alone. Philosophers may certainly dispute this theoretical basis and assumption but at this point and to support the goals of Virternity it is of more primary concern that there is future workability to the mechanism for a transfer of human experience to the virtual realm than necessarily a debate over the actuality of consciousness. It would appear from research by Hayworth in terms of a practical reality that it could be possible in the fullness of time to transfer human memory to computer memory. Potentially this would include some computational ability and thus a form of recorded experience, conscious or otherwise could thus be derived to virtual space. In practical terms, the ultimate goal of the Virternity project, 'Eternal Life', would be within the framework of potential future possibilities although how that 'Eternal Life' is defined will be something for future illumination. Scaling back from this ultimate goal, the project itself consists of a number of milestones the pathway of which should lead to the final vision. The forthcoming series of chapters examines these milestones in more detail in terms of attempting to confirm their basis and validity in terms of research.

Bibliography

Cline, E. (2011). *Ready Player One*. New York: Crown Publishers.

Bailey, D. (2014). *Hyperreality: The merging of the physical and digital worlds* (Masters). University of Brighton.

Baudrillard, J. (1981). *Simulacra and simulation.* Originally published in French by Editions Galilee: Editions Galilee translated into English onto PDF.

Bergson, H., Jacobson, L., & Dingle, H. (1965). *Duration and simultaneity*. Indianapolis: Bobbs-Merrill.

Forster, E. M. (n.d.). *The Machine Stops*. First published in the Oxford and Cambridge Review, November 1909.

Hayworth, K. (2012). ELECTRON IMAGING TECHNOLOGY FOR WHOLE BRAIN NEURAL CIRCUIT MAPPING. *International Journal Of Machine Consciousness*, *04*(01), 87-108. http://dx.doi.org/10.1142/s1793843012400057

Hayworth, K. (2016). *Mind Uploading*. Skeptic, p. 15.

Kassan, P. (2016). *Uploading your mind does not compute*. Skeptic, p. 22.

Leibniz, G., & Strickland, L. (2014). *Leibniz's Monadology* (1st ed.). Edinburgh: Edinburgh University Press.

Wachowski, L., & Wachowski, L. (1999). *The Matrix*. Retrieved from http://www.imdb.com/title/tt0133093/

CHAPTER TWO

Virternity; The goal of setting up a virtual/digital currency - cryptocurrency.

David Evans Bailey

This chapter discusses one of the cornerstones and inception points for the Virternity project, the establishment of a virtual currency. The purpose of this chapter is to delineate the potential advantages and drawbacks regarding the use of a virtual currency as it relates to the Virternity project. It concludes with a brief examination in regard to the feasibility of this aspect of the Virternity project's aims and elements, noting matters which may need to be accounted for in the creation and operation of a virtual currency system.

It is self-evident that any kind of virtual existence which involves the potential transaction of business personal or otherwise will require a method of exchange. Two potential options immediately present themselves in such a scenario. The first would be to continue or attempt to continue the use of the existing banking fraternity and their systems by linking into these with appropriate and proprietary software and interfaces. The second would be to create an independent virtual currency system that does not conform to the conventional fiscal models and is not central bank regulated. It could be considered that the use of the current banking system may not be entirely desirable since one is buying into a heavily regulated institutionalised arena which in itself may exert undue influences on the virtual environment beyond those that are purely financial. If autonomy is sought, then control of financial systems by external institutions and governments is very likely to compromise this aim. One of the key points outlined by the proponents of Virternity is the wish to maintain control by democratic means that is not vested in the hands of one or more individuals, governments or corporations. The creation and use of a virtual currency will distribute and devolve most of the controlling mechanisms for a virtual fiscal system, however, a note of caution must be made to nevertheless consider is whether it can be completely independent of current banking systems and that is certainly a question that will arise. In their discussion paper on virtual currencies, the IMF noted the following points regarding this mode of exchange "*New technologies—supported by advances in encryption and network computing—are driving transformational change in the global economy, including in how goods, services and assets are exchanged. An important development in this process has been the emergence of virtual currencies (VCs). VC schemes are private sector systems that, in many cases, facilitate peer-to-peer exchange bypassing traditional central clearinghouses. VCs and their associated technologies (notably distributed ledgers based on blockchains) are rapidly evolving, and the future landscape is difficult to predict. VCs offer many potential benefits, including greater speed and efficiency in making payments and transfers— particularly across borders—and ultimately promoting financial inclusion. The distributed ledger technology underlying some VC schemes—an innovative decentralized means of keeping track of transactions in a large network—offers potential benefits that go far beyond VCs themselves. At the same time, VCs pose considerable risks as potential vehicles for money laundering, terrorist financing, tax evasion and fraud. While risks to the conduct of monetary policy seem less likely to arise at this stage given the very small scale of VCs, risks to financial stability may eventually emerge as the new technologies become more widely used."* (He et al., 2016, p. 5). The IMF document states that there are clear benefits from a virtual currency system which is decentralised, but it also spells out clear risks associated with an unregulated financial environment of this type. The benefits in speed and efficiency that virtual currency systems can give, allied with the blockchain technology that is used, are one of the attractions for financial markets for this type of instrument. However, concerns regarding issues such as money laundering and fraud, not to mention terrorism, are now genuine concerns in the modern fiscal markets and lack of regulation will signal to some that these risks might then be difficult to mitigate. It is likely that the move towards a fully autonomous VC system would not be popular with the traditional central bank based paradigm albeit that the use of VCs has become an accepted part of the banking scene. The IMF paper continues regarding the value of a virtual currency against that of the traditional fiat currency (a fiat currency is defined as governmentally declared legal tender) *"The value of existing fiat currencies is backed by the creditworthiness of the central bank and the government. Centrally issued VCs rely on the backing of the private issuer's credibility while the value of privately issued currencies... have historically been supported by the private issuer's credibility and commodity reserves. In contrast, the value of cryptocurrencies does not have any backing from any source. They derive value solely from the expectation that others would also value and use them."* (He et al., 2016, p. 9). This points out that the VC system is self-fulfilling in the respect that value derives from those who use it. It is thus not based on the traditional benchmarks of creditworthiness and other current mechanisms in place to determine measures of confidence in matters of currency value and its inherent credibility as a reliable exchange medium. This also indicates that there could be some inherent volatility in a virtual currency since there is no central bank to apply the commonly accepted economic models of fiscal control. The IMF goes on to voice concerns regarding regulation of VCs and indicates that countries are already moving in the direction of introducing legal frameworks for these types of transactions. Latvian Economist Alina Dibrova also echoes these concerns in her paper on virtual currencies where in her first conclusion she asserts *"It has been proved that there is an absolute lack of systematic legislative foundation regulating transactions with virtual currencies. Even more, the approach varies significantly even in the scope of union European market. Such a situation if left neglected might bring new challenges to the market and give a certain support to illegal transactions and money laundering operations."* (Dibrova, 2016, p. 49). She identifies the fact that there are no normative legislative foundations for virtual currencies and their control. Thus, money laundering and illegal monetary transactions are likely to become of concern. She notes that there are significant differences in how these currencies are operated even in a normally regulated market such as the EU. However, she also outlines a more positive view in her second conclusion *"Development of virtual currencies should not be seen purely negative as it might improve the exchange of values among the users. Still, the development of global regulative base should stand prior... The spontaneous end of virtual currency development is very unlikely and therefore, the main challenge is the creation of such climate that would eliminate virtual currency's' possible use in illegal transfers."* (Dibrova, 2016, p. 49). She indicates that VCs can facilitate better exchange methods for users, but for her, the issue of regulation seems of overriding importance. She feels that developing a regulatory framework for these types of currencies is something that should be done prior to their implementation and wider use. Overall these comments illustrate that the concerns regarding virtual currencies revolve not so necessarily around their actual use and creation as much as their potential misuse and therefore the perceived need for regulation. However, within those caveats, there is an implicit and even stated acceptance that VCs have a future and will continue to do so.

The declared aims of Virternity are to provide a new economic and financial system which by implication would be separate from the current governmental and financial institutional models. The initial source of finance would be obtained from private participation and then crowdfunding. It must be conjectured that at some point, particularly in the initial stages it seems very likely that there will need to be, perforce, interfaces to conventional banking systems if only to convert the conventional funding into VC funding. It seems debatable that the total autonomy sought may be initially easy to achieve because of this. There will certainly be a desire for convertible currency transactions to allow crossovers to the banking system and this in itself will introduce regulation. Chartered Accountant Grant Anderson writing for Acuity Magazine has a more pragmatic view of the perceived risks of VCs where he points out that Bitcoin, as an example, is not as anonymous as one might think *"Bitcoin ownership and use is widely thought of as anonymous, which made it popular on 'dark net' websites such as Silk Road (infamous for facilitating drug dealing and other illegal activity). Unfortunately, the perception of anonymity tarnished the image of digital currencies as they appeared to facilitate criminal activity. However, as criminal offenders have found at the cost of their liberty, bitcoin ownership and provenance can be established from the blockchain. Even the UK Treasury acknowledges that Bitcoin is only perceived to be anonymous. More correctly, it can be said to be pseudonymous; ownership is masked to some extent."* (Anderson, 2016, p. 26). This perhaps indicates that some of the fears regarding the anonymity of criminal and other nefarious types of activities that might become associated with digital currencies may not be so well grounded. He notes that the blockchain transaction methods can be used to trace and find offenders, and indeed it has been used in this way. This may be more a function of how the blockchain is used for Bitcoin than a feature of that functionality overall. (Blockchain itself is discussed in more detail in other chapters). In addition, Anderson indicates that Bitcoin is actively traded upon conventional money exchanges *"Bitcoin's volatility as a means of storing value has also drawn a lot of attention. Again, this has tainted many people's views of digital currencies in general. Actually, Bitcoin can be bought and sold like a foreign currency and has a market exchange rate against numerous currencies. There are dozens of active markets and exchanges within which Bitcoin (and* other *digital currencies) can be liquidated and/or converted. The exchange rate of Bitcoin fluctuates in just the same way that exchange rates for sovereign currencies fluctuate."* (Anderson, 2016, p. 26). This point illustrates that autonomy from conventional financial systems may be hard to achieve if it ultimately can be and indeed perhaps it is a feature of financial markets that they will absorb financial instruments into the fold if there is a way of gaining a profit. The fluctuation of exchange rates indicate that active trading is likely to be taking place as this is one of the several factors that can affect rates overall. For the future, Anderson is optimistic in terms of the adoption of digital currencies concluding that *"We have not reached the sweet intersection of consumer acceptance and technological capability for digital currency, but we can't be far from it. The digital wallet technology exists today. Consumer acceptance of digital currencies is growing and will continue to grow. Digital currencies are steadily gaining legitimacy in commerce, courtrooms and legislatures around the world."* (Anderson, 2016, p. 27). His point is that even if the tipping point for wide consumer use of VCs has not been reached, that time is looming closer. His view is that consumers are continuing to accept the use of digital currencies and that they are also being legitimised by other bodies both commercial and legal. Professor of Economics Gerald P. Dwyer also writes in a journal article that *"There is a major difference between digital currency and digital deposits in one respect. The finality of transactions in bitcoins is not guaranteed by an institution such as a bank. Some view this as an advantage but it may not be particularly important to many end users. In other words, there may be little demand for this distinction. To the extent that use of the system requires blind faith in anonymous people's expertise, the complexity is a disadvantage. Furthermore, most people seem to prefer to have their assets and liabilities denominated in the same currency. This reduces their risk in terms of their own currency, which is not trivial given the volatility of exchange rates"* (Dwyer, 2015, p. 90). In effect, he notes that the fact that Bitcoin does not follow the traditional monetary rules in terms of being backed by any fiscal body and that consumers do not seem to find this a drawback. The average person perhaps only requires that the system works and that their own holdings are less exposed to risks of currency fluctuations. This would certainly be true of cross-border holdings where a single virtual currency could be used in two or more countries. In what seems to be an endorsement of virtual currencies Dwyer agrees with other experts in this field, including Anderson, that digital currencies are definitely part of the financial future.

One key element of any type of finance is trust and this is no less the case when it comes to VCs, one might even argue it is of more importance due to the absence of conventional banking endorsement and controls. Finance Professor Luigi Zingales notes the inherent general distrust in finance in a presidential address where he states *"throughout history, finance has been perceived as a rent-seeking activity. Prohibitions against finance date as far back as the Old Testament. The aftermath of the 2007 to 2008 financial crisis has only worsened this view. From Libor fixing to exchange rate manipulation, from gold price rigging to outright financial fraud in subprime mortgages, not a day passes without news of a fresh financial scandal."* (Zingales, 2015, pp. 1327-1328). He refers to the fact that finance itself has never been highly regarded and rather looked upon as a matter of self-interest for the financiers. A number of recent crises have certainly helped to cement the idea in the mind of the public that the banking industry is self-seeking and prone to look after themselves before the customer. In more succinct terms the banking fraternity has sustained a number of events which have damaged the trust that the public has in them. Dr Frens Kreuger defines trust in his paper on 'System Trust' where he notes *"Giddens (1990) connects interpersonal and system trust in the context of a broad historical or "evolutionary" progression. His well-known argument about the development towards (late) modernity shows how virtually all sectors of contemporary organized social life from flying in planes over visiting a doctor to drinking clean tap water fundamentally rely on trust in the respective expert systems, where in pre-modern or early modern times, trust in the individual medic or water-vendor was typically required. The financial sector provides an obvious example for this development. Today, financial markets are regarded as essentially technical phenomena, to be anticipated and engaged with on the basis of rational calculation and largely technical expertise. While this idea has come to be widely taken-for-granted, in the past financial markets used to rely heavily on interpersonal trust."* (Kroeger, 2015, pp. 432-433). Kroeger is alluding to the point that traditional fiscal models are based on trust and personal trust at that. This is perhaps a feature of earlier times when banking was a more personal activity and relationships with the people working at the bank were of primary importance. With the advent of technology and the increasing deferment of decision making to computer-based systems, the need for a personal relationship with bankers has been reduced and the reliance upon fiscal technology has increased. There has been a reversal in effect where trust has been replaced by technological competence in terms of banking systems. The trust element transfers itself to the systems rather than the people who operate and oversee them. The anonymity that inherently accompanies the creation of a VC to a degree dispenses with that trust element. Reliance and trust is therefore heavily founded instead in the robustness and reliability of the technology that underpins it. Thus, a key challenge for the Virternity project is gaining the trust of participants in the virtual currency, its integrity, security and other factors. The underlying technology needs to be extensively 'bullet proof' or resilient in the sense that it cannot fail easily and preferably not at all. When dealing with the matter of personal or even corporate finance, wealth and fortune it is almost a matter of faith that one's currency will be there every time one logs into the computer to check on it or engage in a transaction. Breaking that faith could in effect be catastrophic in terms of the system and confidence in it. Familiarity with current financial systems will need to give way to new ways of working with finance using VCs which are accessible and understandable to the ordinary 'man in the street'. Widespread acceptance will depend ultimately, as Kroeger asserts, upon trust in the system. What can be deduced from his paper is the premise that the system itself must be robust enough to uphold the trust that is placed in it in order to avoid the consequences he otherwise outlines *"the escalating spirals of system trust are balanced on a fine tip; once the underlying basis of system trust is shaken, they can collapse quickly and cataclysmically."* (Kroeger, 2015, p. 435). Thus, he notes that when faith in the system itself is shaken then the trust element is very rapidly lost.

Personal trust has been superseded by technological trust and when that is lost then the breakdown can be catastrophic for financial markets and the fiscal institutions that operate them.

Virternity's intentions to create a new virtual currency to support the new virtual domain relies upon already established precedents in this field and nor is it in doubt that the technology and technical knowhow exists to enable it. What is clear is that the monetary system thus created must hold the confidence and trust of the consumer in order to become ultimately accepted and viable to the aims of the Virternity project. Additionally, interfacing with current financial systems is certainly a factor which is likely to deserve consideration alongside the likelihood and potential for governmental or other types of regulations in various zones across the globe. However, none of those factors need be a barrier to the ultimate success of the Virternity project's aims for a virtual currency creation.

Bibliography

Anderson, G. (2016). New digital money. *Acuity*.

Dibrova, A. (2016). Virtual Currency: New Step in Monetary Development. *Procedia - Social And*

Behavioral Sciences, 229, 42-49.
http://dx.doi.org/10.1016/j.sbspro.2016.07.112

Dwyer, G. (2015). The economics of Bitcoin and similar private digital currencies. *Journal Of Financial Stability, 17*, 81-91. http://dx.doi.org/10.1016/j.jfs.2014.11.006

He, D., Habermeier, K., Leckow, R., Haksar, V., Almeida, Y., Kashima, M., ... Verdugo-Yepes, C. (2016). Virtual Currencies and Beyond: Initial Considerations. INTERNATIONAL MONETARY FUND. Retrieved from https://www.imf.org/external/pubs/ft/sdn/2016/sdn1603.pdf

Kroeger, F. (2015). The development, escalation and collapse of system trust: From the financial crisis to society at large. *European Management Journal, 33*(6), 431-437. http://dx.doi.org/10.1016/j.emj.2015.08.001

Report of the Commonwealth Working Group on virtual currencies. (2016). *Commonwealth Law Bulletin, 42*(2), 263-324. http://dx.doi.org/10.1080/03050718.2016.1195979

ZINGALES, L. (2015). Presidential Address: Does Finance Benefit Society?. *The Journal Of Finance, 70*(4), 1327-1363. http://dx.doi.org/10.1111/jofi.12295

CHAPTER THREE

Virternity; Distributed exchange network: the market without borders

David Evans Bailey

This chapter discusses further the proposal of the Virternity project to establish a virtual currency exchange. It looks at some of the technological definitions and concepts involved and the feasibility of this with due reference to authorities and contemporary thinking on the topic from experts in the field. The Virternity project proposes that a distributed exchange network will allow the users to buy and sell currencies, commodities and services without the use of third-party services, exchange houses and similar mechanisms, which can take advantage of their position. This potentially will facilitate all financial transactions by making them less expensive and more efficient for everyone. In addition to self-benefit, they assert that this market will provide an opportunity to buy and sell coins of the currency the *Virie* directly (not through the stock exchange), making them the easiest to use cryptocurrency.

To address this intention fully requires examination from several different aspects. A previous chapter examined concepts and tenets of virtual currencies and the advantages and some of the disadvantages. As well as this it is necessary to clarify some of the basic starting points and concepts of virtual currency exchange systems. In *The Business Blockchain* (Mougayar & Buterin, 2016), Technology Theorist William Mougayar explains in detail the origins and potential of blockchain technology. It is this technology that will most likely provide the cornerstone for the implementation of a virtual currency in Virternity. Mougayar notes *"The Web could not exist without the Internet. And blockchains could not be without the Internet. The Web made the Internet more useful, because people were more interested in using the information, than figuring out how to hook up computers together. Blockchain applications need the Internet, but they can bypass the Web, and give us* another version that is more decentralized, and perhaps more equitable. That is one of the biggest promises of blockchain technology." (Mougayar & Buterin, 2016, p. 23). This statement implies that blockchain is necessarily prefaced with an accessible working internet or at the very least a distributed network. In effect, blockchain provides a fair distribution of resources across a decentralised network, thus not particularly favouring any one party or location. Going on to outline that cryptography is the basis upon which blockchain transactions are secured Mougayar writes *"Cryptography science is used in multiple places to provide security for a blockchain network, and it rests on three basic concepts: hashing, keys, and digital signatures. A "hash" is a unique fingerprint that helps to verify that a certain piece of information has not been altered, without the need to actually see it. Keys are used in at least a combination of two: a public and a private one... Cryptography is based on the public/private hegemony, which is the yin-yang of the blockchain: public visibility, but private inspection. It's a bit like your home address. You can publish your home address publicly, but that does not give any information about what your home looks like on the inside. You'll need your private key to enter your private home, and since you have claimed that address as yours, no one else can claim a similar address as being theirs.*" (Mougayar & Buterin, 2016, p. 27). This analogy supplies the explanation that in essence a cryptocurrency uses cryptographic or encoded digital fingerprints which can enable a user to locate and verify their own blockchain transactions wherever those transactions are on the network. The keys have two parts one which is public and one private. One allows the public identification of the user but only the private key will allow that user to actually access the information that is stored. The 'hash' is an algorithm applied to a set of numbers which will always produce a certain number or character known as the 'hash'. This 'hash' is a way of verifying that the key is correct and protects against fraud. Further to this concept he then notes "*A blockchain network can validate a variety of value-related transactions relating to digital money or assets that have been digitized. Every time a consensus is reached, a transaction is recorded on a "block" which is a storage space. The blockchain keeps track of these transactions that can be later verified as having taken* place." (Mougayar & Buterin, 2016, p. 32) and then elaborating this idea further *"The blockchain is also a distributed, public, time-stamped asset ledger that keeps track of every transaction ever processed on its network, allowing a user's computer to verify the validity of each transaction such that there can never be any double-counting. This ledger can be shared across multiple parties, and it can be private, public, or semi-private."* (Mougayar & Buterin, 2016, p. 33). The blockchain, as described is, therefore, a chain of actual blocks of transaction data that can be associated across a network and allow the transaction to be verified using, as mentioned, cryptographic keys. The chain of transactions usually contains value related information such as currency amounts. However, because every transaction is recorded there is no erasure or alteration of information and a complete track record of what has taken place is available. Thus, one can conclude that security and protection of identity are not an issue for blockchain. Paola Fico, Head of Primary Markets and Regulatory Compliance provides a more detailed and more technical description of blockchain technology *"VCs exist purely as entries in an accounting system—a transparent* public ledger known as the 'blockchain' that records balances and transfers among special bitcoin 'addresses'. More in detail, a blockchain is a public register or 'distributed ledger' that contains all transactions in the respective virtual currency. At any moment in time the block chain keeps track of who owns how much of the VC. As the word says a block chain is a chain of blocks. The blocks consist of information about several transactions with the virtual currency. Whenever anyone completes a transaction involving a VC this transaction gets logged in a block. Each block contains an identifier of the previous block so that the blocks are linked in a chronological order. Every time a block gets completed a new block is automatically generated. The information contained in a block differs from VC to VC but most seem to contain the following information items: a block number, a 10 time stamp, an identifier of the previous block as a reference, the block's own identifier, at least one transaction, information about the fees/rewards contained in the block. Owning VCs doesn't mean having a digital banknote in a digital pocket; it means having a claim to a bitcoin address, with a secret password, and the *right to transfer its balances to someone else."* (Fico, 2016, p. 4). As he notes, transactions are recorded using what are termed blocks and hence the term 'blockchain' since these are held in a chain. Nominally all blocks within blockchain systems will contain similar types of information to identify them, link them together and allow the values of such things are virtual currencies to be stored. The contents of the chain signify the holdings of that virtual currency for any user which can then be transferred to another user as needed. A transfer will result in another set of blockchain transactions so that the original ones are never lost and the history can always be traced back. The security, integrity, accessibility and the ability to gain access to the blocks in the blockchain at any time are among the key factors in ensuring that it is a workable system. As noted this workability can be in no doubt and is in that sense a proven technology. Traditional EFTPOS based banking systems and electronic ledgers have obviously had many years of development to arrive at the status of a global 24-hour fault tolerant access to financial data. This is naturally a contingent requirement of the globalist culture that is essential in the physical world of high speed transactions which we now inhabit. Any VC system must rapidly assume a similar pedigree in order to become the staple financial exchange medium of the Virternity world, however, the technology of blockchain upon which it is likely to be based has already moved a long way in the direction towards establishing that pedigree.

It is useful to examine the antecedents and provenance of existing virtual currencies and their performance as an exchange system. By reviewing what has been accomplished in this field one can determine how successful VCs which are effectively in circulation already are and what market value they have already achieved. In an article for *Communications of the ACM,* journalist Sara Underwood cites *Michael Versace,* global research director for digital strategies at research firm IDC as relating this significant point about blockchain *"Says Versace, 'The core capabilities of the third platform of technology are beyond any we have seen before. Innovation accelerators like blockchain mean we can achieve technology value outcomes that we couldn't achieve before.'"* (Underwood, 2016, p. 15). Versace implies that blockchain has opened up new outcomes that were not technologically possible before in the field of transaction storage and processing. The article goes on to note that the traditional financial and other types of service providers are showing a growing interest in using blockchain technology, and indicates further how it could be of benefit to developing countries. This is in itself an endorsement of the technology and its future use since robust and reliable fault tolerant systems are the bastion of any financial institution. Professor Marco Iansiti of Harvard University compares the development of blockchain to that of TCIP protocols with similar stages of progress, writing in the *Harvard Review* he says *"Blockchain—a peer-to-peer network that sits on top of the internet—was introduced in October 2008 as part of a proposal for bitcoin, a virtual currency system that eschewed a central authority for issuing currency, transferring ownership, and confirming transactions. Bitcoin is the first application of blockchain technology. The parallels between blockchain and TCP/IP are clear. Just as e-mail enabled bilateral messaging, bitcoin enables bilateral financial transactions. The development and maintenance of blockchain is open, distributed, and shared—just like TCP/IP's. A team of volunteers around the world maintains the core software. And just like e-mail, bitcoin first caught on with an enthusiastic but relatively small community."* (Iansiti & Lakhani, 2017, p. 121). He compares the development of blockchain which was implemented with Bitcoin to that of the networking protocol TCP/IP. This now universal protocol, developed and maintained by volunteering enthusiasts, has become integral to almost all networking software across the world. In the same vein blockchain and Bitcoin had their technological debut but the end result is likely to be that the technology itself will become ubiquitous. He also gives a coherent example of how a stock transaction might work in blockchain technology pointing out its advantages *"In a blockchain system, the ledger is replicated in a large number of identical databases, each hosted and maintained by an interested party. When changes are entered in one copy, all the other copies are simultaneously updated. So, as transactions occur, records of the value and assets exchanged are permanently entered in all ledgers. There is no need for third-party intermediaries to verify or transfer ownership. If a stock transaction took place on a blockchain-based system, it would be settled within seconds, securely and verifiably.*" (Iansiti & Lakhani, 2017, pp. 122-123). This system works upon the principle of multiple identical databases or ledgers which are distributed over a network. The same transaction is recorded in all of the ledgers and due to the way that blockchain works, this is permanent and cannot be erased. Therefore, it removes, in his view, the need for a third party to carry out settlement or change of ownership since this is all contained within the blockchain itself. He points out there are five basic principles that underlie the technology itself: 1) a distributed database which accessible to every party and not controlled by any single party. 2) peer to peer transmission meaning nothing goes through a central node thus again being true distribution. 3) Transparency and pseudonymity where every transaction having a 30-character address is visible to anyone with access to the system and that transactions occur between these addresses. Users may choose to remain anonymous or otherwise. 4) Irreversibility of records meaning that once written a transaction cannot be altered since they are linked, in a chain, to every transaction record that came before them and various algorithms ensure permanency and availability. 5) Computational logic meaning that users can set algorithms and rules to trigger transactions between nodes." (Iansiti & Lakhani, 2017, p. 125). He concludes with this assessment of Bitcoin's potential *"If bitcoin is like early e-mail, is blockchain decades from reaching its full potential? In our view the answer is a qualified yes. We can't predict exactly how many years the transformation will take, but we can guess which kinds of applications will gain traction first and how blockchain's broad acceptance will eventually come about."* (Iansiti & Lakhani, 2017, p. 123). He uses email as an analogy to describe blockchain in its infancy but with the same potential that email had to become universal in its implementation and use. In his estimation, the potential of the technology has not caught up with itself as yet and blockchain has even more to offer. Rob Marvin, editor of PC World in a piece entitled *Blockchain: The Invisible Tech That's Changing the World* writes *"It's important to understand why bitcoin and blockchain are not the same thing. In Garzik's TEDx Talk (https://www.youtube.com/watch?v=vaPgfErzeuO), he described bitcoin as 'an organism.' It has layers, like other software. On top of the bitcoin blockchain is billions of dollars' worth of cryptocurrency, but beneath that is a ledger just like any other blockchain. The underlying ledger works without the currency and can be used to securely transfer any digital asset over the Internet. The currency, on the other hand, doesn't work without the ledger. Garzik said bitcoin was just the first demo application of what blockchain can do. In this case, it built a monetary revolution on the back of an all-seeing ledger, one that's everywhere and nowhere at once, and gave the cryptocurrency its power."* (Marvin, 2017). This assessment of blockchain indicates that Bitcoin's success is due to the technology of blockchain itself. He points out that the two are not synonymous and that one is a virtual currency whilst the other is a technology that supports it. However, this technology could also support any other similar virtual currency and that it is blockchain that empowers those currencies and makes them so effective as financial instruments. We can assume then that without blockchain Bitcoin would not have succeeded. Virternity plans to use blockchain for its own virtual currency and that in itself should provide a measure of the potential success of that currency.

Overall Bitcoin has a track record of 8 years to date and is cited as the example for other virtual currencies to follow. The best indicator of the success of Bitcoin and its underlying technology is the current market value, albeit expressed in US Dollars rather than bitcoin. Sources indicate that in one year it has risen from $5 billion to $14 billion. ("Market Capitalization", 2017). Further, there are 100 or more traded and capitalised cryptocurrencies currently in operation of which Bitcoin is 14 times bigger in terms of capital than its nearest rival Ethereum. ("Crypto-Currency Market Capitalizations", 2017). This current data provides substantial evidence for the proliferation of these types of instruments and provides a good assumption of the confidence participants have in virtual currencies. It is also an endorsement of the blockchain technology that enables them. Peter Lee, Editor of *Euromoney*, casts what must be taken to be a warning note in his article *Banks Take Over the Blockchain* opening his editorial with this statement *"Everything you thought you knew about blockchain is wrong. Rather than wait for the blockchain to re-engineer banking, the banks are going to re-engineer the blockchain. It will not be public, it will be private. And across the shared ledger there will not be that much sharing. In an atmosphere somewhere between excitement and paranoia, banks are trying to turn an existential threat into a competitive advantage"* (Lee, 2016, p. 93). He asserts that blockchain will not be a technology that changes banking technology but rather that banking technology will change some aspects of blockchain to suit themselves. The implication being that big business recognising the value of blockchain technology is moving to make use of it and potentially change the way it works, to their advantage. Further on he notes *"As banks continue to experiment on their own and in collaboration with each other, it seems that many are reaching the same conclusion about transparency - and how unhelpful it can be on the blockchain - that Greenspan identifies. Last year, banks stripped the blockchain away from bitcoin and decided to work on it separately from the cryptocurrency for which it was first built. Now they are decomposing the blockchain itself and searching for ways to keep the benefits of a shared ledger, protected and uncontested, while removing the ability of all participants to see every transaction even if the identities of parties are hidden. Instead of waiting for the blockchain to reshape the banking industry, the banks are reshaping the blockchain."* (Lee, 2016, p. 95). In Lee's view, the banking sector is not entirely comfortable with the protection that blockchain offers to the participants and also the visibility that all participants can have to anything within a blockchain database. Banks are recasting transparency in a less open framework and have even re-engineered the way they deal with Bitcoin. The banking fraternity is altering the way blockchain works to fit the role they want it to fulfil rather than allowing the transaction system to dictate to them a way of working. This is a perfect example as to perhaps why the Virternity project fights shy of using traditional banking and financial participants for their own financial endeavours. Overall Lee notes that the timeframes for usable blockchain proof of concept in the banking industry is 2018 at the earliest moving onwards into 2020, due to the involvement of multiple parties and working groups, regulators and others. Although one could see this move on the part of the financial industry as setting precedents, overall it should not be of undue concern to the Virternity project aiming as it is to work externally to the banking systems and presumably interfacing only where necessary. Given that Virternity whilst distributed in terms of participants is by no means a consortium of corporate interests, it should be able to proceed at a rapid pace building upon what is a proven technology to provide the exchange and virtual currency mechanisms that will facilitate the creation of the virtual world it envisages. Future chapters will discuss more detail regarding the currency model and how this may be achieved based on proven practice in VC operation and technology, they will also examine central banks and other countries approaches and current responses to virtual currencies such as Bitcoin in more depth to establish whether any issues may arise across borders since these may not be of a uniform nature. However, in terms of Virternity's vision of a future distributed exchange network any barriers to its feasibility will tend to lie more in the physical implementation of the technology in terms of the speed that this can be accomplished rather than whether it can be done.

Bibliography

Crypto-Currency Market Capitalizations. (2017). *Coinmarketcap.com.* Retrieved 29 January 2017, from https://coinmarketcap.com/

Fico, P. (2016). Virtual Currencies and Blockchains Potential Impacts on Financial Market Infrastructures and on Corporate Ownership. *SSRN Electronic Journal.* http://dx.doi.org/10.2139/ssrn.2736035

Iansiti, M. & Lakhani, K. (2017). The Truth about Blockchain. *Harvard Business Review.*

Lee, P. (2016). BANKS TAKE OVER THE BLOCKCHAIN. *Euromoney,* (Vol. 47 Issue 566), p92-99, 8p.

Market Capitalization. (2017). *Blockchain.info.* Retrieved 29 January 2017, from https://blockchain.info/charts/market-cap

Marvin, R. (2017). BLOCKCHAIN: THE INVISIBLE TECH THAT'S CHANGING THE WORLD. *PC Magazine,* p91-113, 23p.

Mougayar, W. & Buterin, V. (2016). *The Business Blockchain* (1st ed.). John Wiley & Sons, Incorporated, 2016.

Underwood, S. (2016). Blockchain beyond bitcoin. Communications Of The ACM, *59*(11), 15-17. http://dx.doi.org/10.1145/2994581

CHAPTER FOUR

Virternity; Deposit-Refund System

David Evans Bailey

This chapter discusses further the proposal of the Virternity project to establish a deposit refund system for their virtual currency. It looks at the reasons for this and its feasibility drawing upon authorities and contemporary thinking from experts in the field. The Virternity project proposes that a deposit refund system is required because the deregulated market has already suffered many cases of fraud, dishonesty and lack of guaranties. They suggest that the atmosphere of high risks raises the cost of business operations and this deters potential buyers. In essence, this raises an issue of trust. They argue that their deposit refund system will provide an extra level of security. Virtual transactions would be guaranteed and fraud resistant. The deposit refund system would, therefore, render dishonest conduct of business unprofitable because the fraud will result in a loss to the defrauder due to the refund being carried out.

Some of the issues around the idea of forming a virtual currency and the use of blockchain have been discussed in previous chapters. This chapter intends to focus on the elements of trust that can jeopardize the confidence of consumers in this type of system and touch upon how virtual economies work in practice. The matter of trust and the causes of distrust in banking were outlined in detail in the 2014 publication of their opinion on virtual currencies by the European Central Bank (EBA). Their document states this, among some of the risks to users, which has a particular relevance to the issue at hand *"The risk arises because e-wallets are software that are stored on the user's computer or mobile devices. Those devices might suffer from malfunction as might the software itself. Furthermore, their encryption can be hacked, and unlike a conventional FC, this is possible from anywhere in the world."* In essence the fact that the currency is contained in a digital wallet or storage device which is confined to a particular device and potentially has no backup means that there is very little fault tolerance to the system. It goes on to point out that many VCs do not even have encrypted wallets which may increase the likelihood of hacking which can certainly be agreed would be a definite risk. They also say that users in most of these schemes do not have the right of refund after fraud because the normal banking style safeguards are not in place. The EBA views this as a high priority type of risk, which is to be expected from a banking authority but it could also be looked at from a personal perspective as a client and thus raise concerns that funds, often hard-earned, can be lost in this way. (European Banking Authority, 2014, p. 25). This view does tend to endorse that of the Virternity project in that a deposit refund scheme is needed to mitigate these potential risks. The report goes on to note that because a virtual exchange does not have its own funds, as such, it will lack the resources to refund users, so this would raise another key point to be resolved. Harry Leinonen, advisor to the Bank of Finland, examines the issues surrounding distributed ledger technologies and virtual currencies in a recent paper and what might be considered a key text on this topic where he writes *"Blockchaining and DLT (Distributed Ledger Technology) is simply a* reconciling method for recording in ledgers with decentralised accounts and custodians. This accounting technology can be used for any type of funds. Virtual currencies, Bitcoin, litecoin and peercoin, to name a few, are just specific types of funds, in the same way as euros, dollars or a specific government bond issue are funds. Virtual currencies do not necessarily need to use blockchaining and DLT. It is important to distinguish between the technology used for account keeping in a ledger and the type of funds recorded in that ledger. The situation resembles that of MP3 players as a technology platform that can play any type of music, but are used more for playing the modern music of the younger generation. It is important to clearly separate the technology from the financial content." (Leinonen, 2016, p. 134). His argument is that perhaps the focus on technology has a tendency to override the fundamental principles of maintaining financial ledgers that financial institutions have adhered to almost since their inception. His example referencing MP3 players is an apt one in terms of separating the issues of technology and making the point that financial content and how this is managed is not necessarily a function of technology or rather it illustrates that the technology needs to have the function to support it. He expresses an opinion that blockchain is not a necessity for managing a virtual currency implementation however one might disagree on this simply because the technology is largely proven and has indeed had a long proof of concept with Bitcoin and other virtual currencies. Blockchain would arguably therefore be the technology of choice given its track record and the inherent security features that it does possess. Discussing the concept of banks as custodians of customer funds Leinonen notes this *"Custodians are in charge of maintaining and safekeeping accounts for the owners of the accounts. Banks are the custodians for customers' deposit accounts. Investors' securities accounts are generally kept by custodian banks or special investment service companies. In Bitcoin-type virtual currencies, the starting point has been that the owners of funds themselves act as custodians for their accounts in the same way as for cash."* (Leinonen, 2016, p. 135). He outlines that the duty of banks and other institutions is to maintain deposit account ledgers which are primarily for the safekeeping of the customer's funds and obviously have a secondary regulatory element of compliance with financial services acts in various countries. The fact that Bitcoin types of currencies do not possess this feature implies that the onus is on the consumer to maintain their own custody which can have its own risks depending upon the security of their own computer systems and hardware. Leinonen then indicates *"The most important of the basic additional account information comprises data governing users' (customers') access to their accounts and associated funds. The funds need to be well-protected from unauthorised and fraudulent use by outsiders. The protection needs to be stronger, the larger the balances at stake."* (Leinonen, 2016, p. 135). Blockchain technology in its essence does provide these necessary protections but there is an element of importance in having a recognised way of recording or maintaining what is effectively an impartial and secure ledger of the customer's transactions and balances. A deposit refund system can only function accurately if there is an accurate audit trail to back it up. It is arguable that the blockchain can do this via a transaction by transaction retracing of steps, assuming that this in itself cannot be tampered with. Leinonen also emphasises this aspect *"The technical storage solution of an account is robust when the probability of corrupted or destroyed content is extremely low. High robustness requires secure backups and/or re-creation of account information based, for example, on information available or elsewhere in the ledger. For example, for virtual currencies such as Bitcoin, the infrastructural solution has low robustness as the account safekeeping is delegated to individual account owners acting as custodians without any infrastructural support for backups and re-creation of lost data."* (Leinonen, 2016, p. 135). What he describes is potentially a lack of resilience and fault tolerance in client controlled systems who may not subject their own hardware and data to the rigorous standards of banking service providers. It could be surmised in this way, since the bank offers a service for which they are accountable and can be penalised they will protect the data of their clients in as robust a way as possible, since their own profit lines depend upon it. However, an individual client may not be so careful with their own funds or funds of others that may be hosted on their machines, since the accountability is simply not there. Leinonen also notes that individual transactions in most ledger systems are given a transaction or audit trail number which allows transactions to be identified and traced for reconciliation purposes and where things go wrong, pointing out that traditional systems do already contain many inherent built in safeguards. He goes on to say two things that are different in Distributed Ledger Technology VC transactions *"So what could be new and innovative for DLT-based virtual currencies at the account level? There are two things that differ partly from normal bank account set-ups: account decentralisation to consumer-level custodians and stronger cryptography."* (Leinonen, 2016, pp. 135-136). These are important issues and very much a feature of blockchain systems. As noted above, Leinonen himself points out the fragility of security of the average user's home computer and its vulnerability to hacking and that most home computer users will need to purchase or install proprietary software to secure their own ledgers and transactions. He also says that there are specialised virtual currency custodians already arising in the market who offer a more secure way of holding and securing customer deposits. Leinonen further discusses that although VC's have PKI (Public Key Infrastructure) technology the weakness still rests with client computers holding the information and asserts *"Virtual currency schemes have been some years ahead of traditional payment services in implementing PKI-based encryption, but there is still a need for security improvements in both. Both traditional and novel payment systems face the same need to implement improved security features to keep up with e-criminals stepping up their e-robbing methods."* (Leinonen, 2016, p. 136). Unlike banks who have secure firewalled fault tolerant systems, blockchain distributed networks may not have the benefit of these secure and resilient features. Whilst Leinonen debates the fact that ledgers can be centralised or decentralised, and that the reconciliation process is essentially the same regardless apart from a time element, how the Virternity currency system will deal with reconciliation will need to be addressed and answered specifically. Currently the indications are that there will not be a central or decentralised ledger within the Virternity currency system. He also emphasises that virtual currencies are just what the name implies, they are not security backed and they are perpetual instruments which are issued anonymously without any institution regulating monetary policy when compared to traditional monetary systems. In conclusion, he ultimately sits on the fence regarding the long-term success of VC systems. Dr Max Kubat writing for the University of Economics in Prague analyses Bitcoin as money and also finds some flaws *"Contemporary monetary theories use, next to theoretical definition of money, empirical definition because the theoretical definition is limited to legal money too. The aim of the empirical definition of money is to deal with the relationship between quantitative development of money and other macroeconomic variables. Therefore, in addition to the definition of money, it copes with the question what money is and what is not in circulation... In the case of Bitcoin, the empirical definition is again in serious trouble. It is clear what is and what is not bitcoin. Given that, Bitcoin is not significantly associated with banking system, there is no such thing as Bitcoin term deposits or securities issued in Bitcoin. Bitcoin can be used at any time and therefore differentiation according to the levels of liquidity is meaningless. Bitcoin can be in terms of liquidity equated to money on current accounts in banks, more precisely with regard to speed of the*

bitcoins transfers we can talk about a "virtual cash"."
(Kubát, 2015, p. 144). He is critical overall of Bitcoin because it doesn't conform to accepted rules of monetary systems and asserts that it does not meet the usual criteria of money in current financial models. What he is really saying is that in his view money has a more complex relationship than simply exchange of goods, it is affected by variables in the economy on a macro scale which may imply that sectors of financial investment or spending will, as one commonly sees, affect the value of currency, and naturally interest rates that are imposed by central banks. Bitcoin doesn't have any securities or deposits as such and that makes it more of an exchange system than a traditional banking system, it is not a system for investment *per se*. That is however not to say that virtual currencies should have to meet these criteria, rather one could envisage an opportunity to change to paradigm which is after all one of the stated ambitions of Virternity itself. Viternity is entering what is effectively a new playing field in terms of virtual reality and a virtual life, therefore the need to apply normal rules of engagement in terms of finance should certainly be questioned, if not challenged. The irony is that current financial

systems are the only benchmark that one can apply in evaluating the case, if for no other reason than to supply a list of challenges that must be overcome.

To further examine the concept of deposits and indeed the currency system it is advisable to take a brief look at virtual economies in action. In a short paper, Nazir and Lui from James Cook University examined the idea of virtual economy in virtual worlds. Their analysis looked at a number of virtual worlds such as *Second Life* and *World of Warcraft* in terms of the economy thus created. Their examination noted the proliferation of real estate sales within some of these worlds, as well as the fact that an abortive attempt to set up a bank in *Second Life* had resulted in those participants being banned. They also note the most common type of virtual currency transactions as follows *"Exchanging virtual currency with virtual goods is the most common type of VE transaction. Users can purchase virtual goods - including clothes, cars, furniture, and pets - with virtual currency. These virtual goods can then be delivered digitally to the avatar representing the users in virtual world. Users can also pay for virtual services such as real estate, education, health care, and governmental services."* (Nazir & Lui, 2016,

p. 11). It might be expected that this would be a similar case in Virternity. They write that a number of well known brands also sell virtual and some physical goods via these virtual worlds. Of notable interest is the fact that most worlds initiate their currency transactions via real world currency conversions to the virtual currency before making purchases in the virtual currency. However, this is more a symptom of the fact that the virtual worlds examined are an addendum to the physical world rather than a replacement. In the sense that Virternity ultimately aims to become a replacement for some participants thus forsaking the physical world entirely, then the incorporation or at least simulation of financial practice in the world of Virternity is likely to be necessary. Indeed, this very fact of policy and economics is ably discussed by Edward Castronova Professor of Telecommunications at Indiana University Bloomington in a wide-ranging dissertation on the virtual economies of virtual worlds he emphatically concludes *"Traditionally, virtual worlds have attempted to insulate themselves from the policy issues of the real world by defining themselves as spaces for play, enclosed in a magic circle. The role of world-makers as governments was* recognized very early in the history of virtual environments, but was considered from the start as completely distasteful and unfortunate...The social world of humanity creates policymaking jobs and, if it must, imposes them on specific people to handle as best they can. These same forces have created policymaking positions in the leadership of virtual world making companies... The reality of economics is that whenever the necessary conditions exist – a group of people with some process for moving, storing, and recording the location and ownership of goods – an economy based on real value is certain to follow. While part of the erosion of the magic circle has occurred because of the inevitable consequence of economies emerging under the necessary conditions and communities demanding governance, developers have also encouraged erosion by crafting new revenue models and managing worlds as if they were policy makers. As developers continue to impose themselves as the policy makers of virtual worlds with real consequences for ethics, law, and government we imagine that a collision between virtual policy makers and real world policy makers is inevitable."* (Castronova, Knowles, & Ross, 2015, p. 794). The implication of what could be viewed as a quite profound statement is that virtual world makers cannot escape the need for their own rules and policy within their world. It is almost *de facto* that they will have to set up their own policies to manage the domains over which they preside. One might imply therefore and argue counter to a previous point and say that perhaps the paradigm of a virtual existence cannot be changed as much as one might hope. It is more of a question perhaps of how much it is possible to reinvent society and accepted ways of commerce. What Castronova notes from his study is that makers of virtual worlds begin with intentions to effect a hands-off approach to the world, its governance and economy and soon discover that this is impractical, if not impossible, to achieve in reality. The virtual world is still populated by real people behind the avatars who will more than likely behave in social patterns and mores that are similar to those they are already engaging in their physical existence. The expectation that people will change to a new way of living and working is perhaps not as easy to effect as one might consider. There is evidently a fine line dividing what is desired and what can be achieved in this regard. The experiences of other virtual world creators are something that the Virternity project could learn valuable lessons from and perhaps it could be helpful to examine real-world models for solutions particularly when at the starting point of something entirely new.

To summarise it is useful to examine a view of the most successful virtual currency so far. Pavel Ciaian from the European Commission writes in a paper, debating whether Bitcoin can become a global currency *"The use of BitCoin in market exchanges bears a certain risk, because of the absence of any protection against disputes between parties involved in the exchange. Once a BitCoin transaction is realized, it is irreversible and cannot be disputed. There is no centralized mechanism available to revert an erroneous transaction or to handle the disputes with the aim to provide protection against human errors of fraud that may occur in exchanges (e.g. protection against disputes over non-fulfillment of contract). Currently, the correction of an erroneous transaction is possible only through a voluntary agreement of the parties involved in the exchange (EBA 2014 ; Bo¨hme et al. 2015). We may conclude that the absence of an institution regulating and enforcing BitCoin related disputes, the popularity and use of BitCoin as a currency may be impeded, particularly for risk-averse market participants."* (Ciaian, Rajcaniova, & Kancs, 2016, p. 893). This point noting that Bitcoin has not resolved the opportunity to refund investors or resolve issues over payments between parties is among several issues that Ciaian examines in his paper but is arguably one of the most relevant and important to this topic. What it particularly highlights is the fact that Bitcoin, the current premiere virtual currency, has not resolved the problem of disputes and refunds satisfactorily if at all and thus does not put forward an example of a virtual currency doing this which can be followed or examined. Rather the opposite it leaves the deposit and refund issue open-ended. This is in effect an opportunity now open to Virternity to resolve with their own offering. There is little doubt that being able to put workable solutions in place for this would lift the Virternity currency above its contenders and into the premiere spot where it wants to be positioned. Ciaian concludes that Bitcoin may nevertheless have advantages in developing countries and as a remittance system *per se,* but shies away from an outright endorsement of Bitcoin, rather stating the pros and cons of the proposition. He praises blockchain as opening up many possibilities in terms of financial and technologically linked innovations and finishes with this positive statement which is very *apropos* to the Virternity project itself *"Further, the disruptive innovation of BitCoin provides the potential to give citizens direct control over their financial activities by removing costly—and sometimes obscure— intermediation layers fostering financial inclusion."* (Ciaian, Rajcaniova, & Kancs, 2016, p. 917). With which statement he seems to imply that the attractiveness of a virtual currency system is that it removes the intermediaries such as banks and other financial institutions and this is a move which could be seen as giving back control to the people.

It can be concluded that blockchain technology is a proven method of running a virtual currency system and this is not in doubt. However, wider issues remain regarding security and robustness of the transactions once stored. Virternity wants to move away from traditional banking paradigms to a distributed ledger style of system. As outlined in this chapter there are some potentially significant drawbacks to this in terms of security of customer information where it may have been altered or tampered with. Without a centralised ledger, these issues become more complex. However, it is most likely that intermediaries and exchanges will arise that will allow customers to hold their funds in a more secure framework and one where they can fully trust the information and this in itself would more easily facilitate a deposit refund system. To engage in a refund system based on a Bitcoin style of entirely distributed transactions may otherwise require some very sophisticated and robust tracking techniques to enable facilities such as refunds to be accomplished. That is to not say this is impossible or even improbable, but rather to point out that there are issues and solutions that will need due consideration before implementation. Having laudable aims is one thing, carrying them out is another. To borrow the title of the famous novel by writer Aldous Huxley (1931), the designers of Virternity must face these challenges in the creation of their own *'Brave New World'*.

Bibliography

Castronova, E., Knowles, I., & Ross, T. (2015). Policy questions raised by virtual economies.

Telecommunications Policy, 39(9), 787-795.
http://dx.doi.org/10.1016/j.telpol.2014.12.002

Ciaian, P., Rajcaniova, M., & Kancs, d. (2016). The digital agenda of virtual currencies: Can BitCoin become a global currency?. *Information Systems And E-Business Management, 14*(4), 883-919. http://dx.doi.org/10.1007/s10257-016-0304-0

European Banking Authority. (2014). *EBA Opinion on 'virtual currencies'*. EBA.

Kubát, M. (2015). Virtual Currency Bitcoin in the Scope of Money Definition and Store of Value. *Procedia Economics And Finance, 30*, 409-416. http://dx.doi.org/10.1016/s2212-5671(15)01308-8

Leinonen, H. (2016). Virtual currencies and distributed ledger technology: What is new under the sun and what is hyped repackaging?. '*Journal Of Payments Strategy & Systems, 10*(2), 132-152.

Nazir, M. & Lui, C. (2016). A Brief History of Virtual Economy. *Journal Of Virtual Worlds Research, 9*(1).

CHAPTER FIVE

Virternity: Iris Scan Access for Secure Access

David Evans Bailey

This chapter discusses further the proposal of the Virternity project to use iris scan technology to enable secure access to the Virternity systems and assets. Current developments and the technology itself are examined as well as future potentials.

Iris scan technology is no longer part of science fiction folklore and has been around for quite some time. Although iris scanning cannot be currently held to be mainstream in terms of access technology, it certainly is a field where developments are likely to bring it into more and more use within the public domain. It would be useful to examine how the technology itself works and also why it should be considered secure. Iris scans are considered accurate forms of biometrics and unlike fingerprints, they do not wear with age. The iris can be rapidly scanned and matched. It must be understood that an iris is the coloured ring of tissue around the eye pupil and irises are unique to individuals even though the colours are complex. The scanning works in two parts; the first being the identification of unique traits within the iris and the second their subsequent analysis. For example, the Samsung Note 7 uses both infrared and normal cameras for scanning and identifies at least 240 iris features which is five times the detection rate of fingerprint scanners. An iris code is created from this scan against which identification is then possible. ("How phone Iris Scanners Work", 2016). Thus, iris scanning is a two-step process, the first is the formation and registration of the iris code and the second is the matching of this code when the user attempts to use functions protected by this feature. It can be considered to be several steps up from a normal password type of security system. A recent paper surveying the field of Ocular Biometrics notes that Infra-Red recognition systems are more reliable than normal visual range spectrum cameras particularly in low lighting conditions and this should be something to take into consideration when opting for a technology within the field of VR. Obviously, it is important that this kind of technology is as fool proof as possible in terms of making positive identifications and also in the reliability of the system. When wearing a typical VR headset there is also no internal illumination. Researchers Ajita Rattani and Reza Derakhshani write *"Typically, iris recognition systems operate under NIR illumination with wavelengths ranging between 700 nm to 900 nm. Under NIR illumination, the effect of melanin is negligible. Therefore, operating at NIR spectrum ensures that the acquired image reveals information related to the texture rather than pigmentation. The nuances of the iris texture of dark-colored irides are much better observed in the NIR spectrum"* (Rattani & Derakhshani, 2017, p. 3). Their paper also notes that studies have identified that iris recognition systems typically degrade under visual light due to such issues as focusing problems, motion blur and variations in illumination, although software algorithms have been built by a number of parties that mitigate these issues since evidently, the use of infrared is not always possible. As noted, however, in the realm of immersive VR technology visual light could not be used and infrared is the only realistic option. A number of systems are now using the conjunctival vasculature as the effective data source for eye scans instead of the iris itself. *"The conjunctiva is a thin, transparent, and moist tissue that covers the outer surface of the eye. The ocular conjunctiva is very thin and clear; thus the surface vasculature (due to conjunctiva and episclera) are easily visible through it. The visible micro-circulation of conjunctiva and episclera offers a rich and complex network of veins and fine micro-circulation."* (Rattani & Derakhshani, 2017, pp. 4-5). According to Rattani's paper, these systems use the blood vessels in the white of the eye as opposed to the iris and they are captured as the eye moves from left to right. The vessels and patterns contained in the whites of the eye are also unique to each individual. This could be an alternative method of secure identification and could possibly be considered against the more traditional iris methods because they also have the advantage of being hard to spoof. This method at the moment uses the visible light spectrum however which would be an issue when using VR headsets. From their study, it appears that the rapidly developing field of iris recognition overall needs continued focus on good hardware to facilitate image capture since the quality of the image itself dictates to some degree the reliability of the system in terms of secure and correct identification of individuals using this means.

It is useful to examine the progress of iris scan technology within society currently. An article in *The Verge* notes that the San Bernadino Sherriff's department was collecting around 189 iris scans per day in 2016 as part of a pilot project *"San Bernardino's activity is part of a larger pilot program organized by the Federal Bureau of Investigation, one that began as a simple test of available technology but has quietly grown into something far more ambitious. Since its launch in 2013, the program has stockpiled iris scans from 434,000 arrestees, an FBI spokesperson confirmed."* (Lecher, 2015). The article notes that these scans are being shared with other agencies such as the US Border Patrol in what appears to be a systematic effort to introduce yet another means of identifying individuals in society and it might be surmised particularly 'persons of interest'. This technology makes the collection of this particular biometric information faster and potentially easier than traditional methods such as fingerprints. Once scans have been made then the practical implications of using them in various facilities and for example, for roadblocks are noted and naturally with all the concerns that could be had in terms of individual privacy. The implications and matters of concern are not least on account of the fact that the development of long distance iris scanning has been in progress since 2015 as an article in *The Conversation* by two research fellows suggests *"Biometric technologies are on the rise. By electronically recording data about individual's physical attributes such as fingerprints or iris patterns, security and law enforcement services can quickly identify people with a high degree of accuracy. The latest development in this field is the scanning of irises from a distance of up to 40 feet (12 metres) away. Researchers from Carnegie Mellon University in the US demonstrated they were able to use their iris recognition technology to identify drivers from an image of their eye captured from their vehicle's side mirror." (Oostveen & Dimitrova, 2015).* It is understandable that perhaps there may be alarm in some quarters with which this particular development would be received. The potential for tracking individuals across a wide swathe of public areas becomes effectively possible once the recognition databases are in place. In fact, surveillance camera systems are already prevalent across multiple locations and countries all over the globe, so their secondary use for this would be easy to effect. Citizens would have a right to be concerned that their anonymity would be almost constantly breached if this kind of system were put into wider use and perhaps there is an inevitability about that consequence which is not the subject of this chapter. However, the introduction of this type of identification system into a VR universe such as Virternity does pose a number of implications which mirror concerns that would be present in the physical world. The idea of an easy system of identification and access to all resources within the VR domain would be attractive to users but on the other side there is the privacy issue and once a person is thus identified then anonymity is no longer necessarily an option. Effectively once registered on the system and identified then the user can be tracked wherever they are in the virtual realm. Arguably though this in itself is inherent within the system regardless of what type of identification is used because, in order to access the system and draw down the personal attributes of their identity, an individual would require some type of secure access. The advantage of using iris scanning would be that people could be more secure in the knowledge that identity theft or the possibility of someone else using your online profile would be much lower than having only a password protection type of system. This kind of identity theft or use of another's profile would obviously be a concern for those in a world such as Virternity.

The history of iris recognition goes back more than ten years of provenance. Three years ago, in their *Handbook of Iris Recognition*, scientists Kevin Bowyer and Mark Burge noted *"A recent survey of iris biometric research from its inception through 2007, roughly 15 years of research, lists approximately 180 publications..."* and they go on to say that it is a rapidly expanding field with many practical applications illustrating the use of this technology (Bowyer & Burge, 2013, p. 15). In 2004, Professor John Daugman, who is considered one of the foremost original developers of this technology, wrote a paper on iris recognition where he presented the results of tests using algorithms that he had developed *"This paper explains the iris recognition algorithms and presents results of 9.1 million comparisons among eye images from trials in Britain, the USA, Japan, and Korea."* (Daugman, 2004, p. 21). He noted that there were no false matches in any of these tests proving the reliability of the techniques and the technology itself even at those early stages. Bowyer and Burge, however, write in their book that open research issues do exist around, for example, wearers of contact lenses which although solved to an extent by Daugman did not do so for all types of contact lenses. They also point out that other types of lens artefacts and even damage to pupils or irregularities in the eye itself can also cause problems for identification. (Bowyer & Burge, 2013, pp. 2-7). The conclusion from these findings are that whilst iris recognition technology has been developing for some time and is coming into increasing use, there are still issues that need to be ironed out for the future. The incorporation of eye tracking into VR headsets has already begun according to *CNET* earlier in 2016 with an article that noted: *"Two separate companies at Mobile World Congress in Barcelona this week showed off modified Oculus and Samsung Gear VR headsets with built-in eye-tracking capabilities."* ("Eye tracking in VR headsets is the future, and it's starting now", 2016). Thus, illustrating that this feature is already on the VR horizon incorporating new features and innovations. Another headset, albeit not mainstream, is the *FOVE*, a Californian offering with built-in eye tracking and which bills this as a feature. In the company's blog, they cite their origins thus *"FOVE began from the University of Tokyo's academic collaboration facility in Tokyo, Japan, and development is being carried out one of Japan's top hardware laboratories. We are committed to incorporating the latest VR technology, with cooperation from Asian hardware manufacturers such as Toshiba and Samsung."* ("Home - FOVE Eye Tracking Virtual Reality Headset", 2017). With built-in infrared scanning this technology already offers the reliability of this method eye and iris scanning mentioned above and is no doubt pitched to provide features that other current market leaders such as Vive and Oculus do not incorporate into their products without modification. However, there are suppliers in the marketplace who already offer these features as hardware add-ons to those particular headsets. It can, therefore, be certain in terms of feasibility that as far as Virternity is concerned the technological needs of iris recognition can be and will be met in the scope of the VR arena.

To complete the examination of this topic requires a brief look at the security of iris recognition technology in terms of how easy it is to fool it. The accepted terminology for this is 'spoofing' and there are different ways in which attempts can and have been made to do so. Bowyer and Burge devote a chapter to this which includes their own research, their technique involves isolating the discriminating pattern for an individual's iris and then embedding this unique iris code pattern into a different person's iris so that it can be recognised. Using the combined patterns in the new iris they then attempted recognition to see if the identity could be spoofed. In conclusion to this research, they write *"we explored a method of creating spoof irises to aid an imposter in bypassing an iris recognition system. We showed how such a spoof pattern of a 'genuine' person may be generated using knowledge of only his/her iris bit code template and knowledge of the Gabor parameters used by the iris recognition system. The results in the previous section show natural-looking spoof iris images (spoof pattern* embedded within another's iris image) which give similar verification performances as the genuine pattern when presented to the recognition system." (Bowyer & Burge, 2013, pp. 356-364). How easy a spoof would be to create based on these techniques is a matter of debate but the experiments show that it can be done and thus iris recognition is not entirely fool proof. In an article for *Forbes* magazine in 2015 security researcher Jan Krissler also claims to be have been able to 'hack' iris recognition technology using 4k images of famous politicians gleaned from the internet. The article says *"In his tests in December, Krissler messed with Panasonic's Authenticam BM-ET200 iris recognition technology, a product that has been discontinued but the only system he said he has seen in common use today."* (Fox- Brewster, 2015). There is also some debate to be had regarding these claims, which to a degree centre around the technology that was used and the fact that technology is and has improved since that date, and indeed will be improving all the time. In a paper reviewing iris recognition, anti-spoofing members of the Biometric Recognition Group-ATVS, Javier Galbally and Marta Gomez-Barrero point out that three types of spoofing are recognised; photos, contact lenses (with a printed fake iris pattern) and artificial eyes (made of plastic or glass). Current techniques are discussed, such as those which measure the 'aliveness' of the eye in terms of reflex actions such as pupil dilation which would automatically detect a static image type of spoof. Other ways of detection include features analyses which can use the binary patterns and compare them to known spoofing types of artificially created or photographic patterns. In summary, they note *"To conclude, we can say that, as the article has shown, big advances have been achieved in the development of countermeasures against attacks to the sensor. However, every day new attacking methodologies are also being devised in order to gain fraudulent access to the information protected by these systems."* (Galbally & Gomez-Barrero, 2016). Thus, having identified the main forms of 'attack' and discussed defences against them it is clear that advances have been made in detection of spoofing attempts. They counsel that the research and development in this area must continue as spoof attacks become more sophisticated. That, however, is only to be expected in any security technology and it is only necessary to cite the example of computer virus detection to show this to be true.

In conclusion, Virternity has the means to fulfil its security ambitions in terms of iris recognition. The hardware and software advances are continuing and this type of technology has become more prevalent and thus accepted in society. There are inevitable caveats that must accompany any security based system which centre around privacy, reliability and indeed how secure they really are. With the right technical teams in place, there should be no barriers to Virternity's implementation of this technology nor can there be doubts about its effectiveness as a secure method of access to the Virternity systems when these finally arrive.

Bibliography

Bowyer, K. & Burge, M. (2013). *Handbook of Iris Recognition* (1st ed.). London: Springer London.

Daugman, J. (2004). How Iris Recognition Works. *IEEE Transactions On Circuits And Systems For Video Technology*, 14(1), 21-30. doi:10.1109/tcsvt.2003.818350

Eye tracking in VR headsets is the future, and it's starting now. (2016). *CNET*.

https://www.cnet.com/news/eye-tracking-vr-headsets-future-mwc-virtual-reality-oculus-samsung-gear/

Fox-Brewster, T. (2015). *Forbes Welcome. Forbes.com.* http://www.forbes.com/sites/thomasbrewster/2015/03/05/clone-putins-eyes-using-google-images/#352621984f85

Galbally, J. & Gomez-Barrero, M. (2016). A review of iris anti-spoofing. *2016 4Th International Conference On Biometrics And Forensics (IWBF).* doi:10.1109/iwbf.2016.7449676

Home - FOVE Eye Tracking Virtual Reality Headset. (2017). *FOVE Eye Tracking Virtual Reality Headset.* https://www.getfove.com/

How phone Iris Scanners Work. (2016). *The Press,* A14.

Lecher, C. (2015). *The FBI has collected 430,000 iris scans in a so-called 'pilot program'. The Verge.* http://www.theverge.com/2016/7/12/12148044/fbi-iris-pilot-program-ngi- biometric-database-aclu-privacy-act

Oostveen, A. & Dimitrova, D. (2015). *Iris scanners can now identify us from 40 feet away. The Conversation.* https://theconversation.com/iris-scanners-can-now-identify-us-from-40- feet-away-42141

Rattani, A. & Derakhshani, R. (2017). Ocular biometrics in the visible spectrum: A survey. *Image And Vision Computing, 59,* 1-16. doi:10.1016/j.imavis.2016.11.019

CHAPTER SIX

Virternity: Connection of augmented and virtual realities. Emergence of the shareable compound reality = Virternity fully-featured space

David Evans Bailey

This chapter discusses further the proposal of the Virternity project to mix augmented and immersive technologies and the resulting realities into a compound shared reality. The progress of these technologies to date will be examined together with future prospects and what the feasibility is for this ultimate goal being realised.

It is important to summarise the current state of play with respect to various known VR technologies. VR is currently split between two types of technology; immersive technology and augmented reality technology. It might be said that the two streams are progressing in tandem although advances in immersive technology currently outstrip the augmented version just in terms of what is commercially available in the public domain. Investment in both types of technology is high and prominent companies in the field are involved in either one or both of these areas. It cannot be known at this time whether a point of mergence or indeed rivalry between the two technologies is necessarily envisaged. To date, the market is dominated by immersive headsets and sales figures reflect this; Samsung, Playstation, Vive and Oculus are the front runners. In China a different set of low-cost headsets and mobile VR are popular. ("Best Branded Google VR Cardboards", 2017). The sales of immersive technology are significant but possibly not as high as was envisaged by industry pundits at the beginning of 2016. One reason cited for the relatively low sales figures compared to predictions through 2016 are that the headsets and associated hardware are relatively costly and also the lack of a VR style of 'blockbuster' to encourage the take-up of hardware in large numbers. The claim is that higher sales will also encourage developers to invest more money in software to run on the platforms. (Brewster, 2017). The argument could become circular if developers are waiting on sales of hardware before investing their time and energy into making software for it. It is more likely that the sales and release of new software will continue on a slow steady rise. The number of technology users is a major factor in influencing the success of VR platforms and potentially VR worlds such as Virternity. To attract more users requires affordable technology and also software or VR experiences that interest people at large. The use of VR is spread across many different fields which include medicine, sport and education as well as leisure based activities. However, there is no doubt that participation on a wide scale requires something that will draw people into using it as, for example, with smartphone technology social applications such as Facebook ensured a rapid take-up. In fact, Facebook has recently launched an app as a beta product called 'Spaces' which marries immersive

VR technology with a 360 camera and thus mixes the real world and the VR world together as one. Avatars of people are mixed with scenes of their actual location but also augmented by virtual objects, menus and so forth. A recent article in *Wired* magazine noted *"When you launch Spaces from within your Oculus Rift headset, though, it logs into your Facebook account. The same one that you, along with nearly 2 billion other people on the planet, use on a regular basis."* (Rubin, 2017). It remains to be seen whether this mix of augmented and immersive VR realities is going to take off with consumers but the fact that Facebook is investing in such an application is a good indication of its likely success. If such platforms are being built which then become popular this will increase the use of VR technology overall and for the Virternity project this would certainly be a positive development.

As far as augmented reality is concerned, it is fair to say that this has yet to become a mainstream product. Apple CEO Tim Cook predicts *"VR experiences will be an integral part of our daily lives, comparing the emerging technology to the iPhone and eating three meals a day."* And he goes on to say that we will wonder how we ever did without it. (Raymundo, 2016). Apple is investing in AR as a future product albeit it at the 'baby steps' stage as the author of the article describes it. However, it is of significance that a company whose revenue exceeds $200 billion per year is engaging with this particular technology and augers for its likely future success. Joining this high-profile company are Microsoft with *HoloLens* an AR headset currently undergoing testing with business users and selected customers but with a significant price tag of $3000 and Magic Leap with what is apparently a retinal projection AR headset that is still in development. Predictions are still that *"for the average person without a big budget and the willingness to tinker with a technology still under development, AR heavy remains somewhere beyond the horizon."*(Perry, 2017, p. 39). That is the conclusion of one expert who however notes that *Pokémon Go* an AR style of game has nevertheless had an amazing run of success in spite of the actual AR hardware not having been fully developed as yet. With such participation and an appetite from consumers, AR will challenge the VR market at some future point. One of the reasons for this may be that AR does not require full immersion and thus implied disconnection from the physical world. Whilst this aspect may be desirable for some because they perhaps enjoy the physical isolation, the idea that a person can experience both the digital and physical worlds at the same is likely to be an attractive proposition albeit perhaps technologically harder to achieve.

When referring to mixed reality as a medium it should be more correctly noted that it is actually a version of augmented reality. Some will also refer to AR as simply being a way of adding digital content using a smartphone. *Pokémon Go* is an example of this, where GPS tracking is used to locate *Pokémon* that are digitally placed in locations around the world. The user has to walk to the location the physical world and then catch the *Pokémon* using the app on the smartphone. The *HoloLens* goes beyond this idea and is a version of AR where holographic images are projected in front of the person and thus viewed as if they are part of the physical world. This mixed reality scenario is the ultimate aim of Virternity where participation would only be partially immersive as opposed to fully immersive. In his article *"The HoloLens Revolution"*

Eminent Scholar Ahmed K. Noor indicates that this product is being extensively used by NASA already *"Another NASA application called ProtoSpace uses holograms for spacecraft design. The system superimposes a computer generated version of space hardware over the field of view of the user's headset."* This he says enables engineers to walk around full-scale versions of the spacecraft and thus test fit virtual components. Other NASA applications include the superimposition of animated holographic illustrations over equipment that space crew are working on. (Noor, 2016, p. 33). The article illustrates the fact that holographic types of displays that facilitate the mixed reality scenario are rapidly moving beyond the development stage. In the not too distant future, these will be released into the public domain. In fact, Noor, a professor of modelling and simulation, believes that ultimately these will be capable of rendering 3D content that blends seamlessly with the environment and that the headsets will be light enough to wear continuously. (Noor, 2016, p. 34). For some proponents of the field, the future of mixed reality is a bright one. In 2015 researchers Ricci et al. wrote a discussion of mixed reality living. In this paper, they proposed the idea of large-scale smart environments which would then support city-wide tracking and augmented reality. They discuss the idea of mirror worlds *"In the mirror world vision, smart spaces are modeled in terms of digital cities shaped by the physical world with which they're coupled, inhabited by open societies and organizations of software agents playing the role of the inhabitants of those cities."* (Ricci, Piunti, Tummolini, & Castelfranchi, 2015, p. 62). They go on to note that this may eventually change human cognitive function as it combines with the artificially created digital world. In other words, people will use the intelligence and capabilities of AR to enhance their capabilities of analysing data and situations and making decisions. It would be, in effect, a step above simply consulting Google for additional information but instead adding the capabilities of artificial intelligence to human intelligence. Mirror worlds were first mooted by artist and scientist David Gelertner (1992) in which he expounded the theories of software being capable of producing AR and the impact that this might have. Twenty-five years later technology is on the brink of fulfilling some of these predictions. Virternity may well be the world that will complete this vision.

In an article for *Forbes*, writer David Ewalt says of the technology under development by Magic Leap *"Neither a VR game nor Pokémon Go can do what Magic Leap's 'mixed reality' does. VR takes you to another place. AR can make a Pikachu appear in your living room. Mixed reality keeps you where you are and makes that Pikachu come to life... when you're wearing the device, it doesn't block your view of the world; the hardware projects an image directly onto your retina through an optics system built into a piece of semitransparent glass...The hardware also constantly gathers information, scanning the room for obstacles, listening for voices, tracking eye movements and watching hands. As a result, mixed-reality objects are aware of their environment and have the ability to interact with the real world."* (Ewalt, 2016, p. 79). Investment in this product has been in the hundreds of millions of dollars to date with stakes taken by Google and other blue-chip investors. According to the article, the product uses a 'photonic chip' which allows images to bounce off it and directly into the retina of the eye, the system uses the brain to process these images and that is partly why they are so realistic in appearance. If Magic Leap does indeed live up to its advertised capabilities, then it could change the reality paradigm in the future. It is likely that Magic Leap and *HoloLens* will release to the public later in 2017. At this point what is currently only the potential of mixed reality will become actual fact for the masses as opposed to only a select few. It is impossible to assess the impact that this will have but it can certainly be conjectured that it is going to be of great significance in time. The rapidity of the AR's take-up will naturally depend upon the price and the availability of applications appealing to the mass market as well as specialised areas. Whether it is likely to lead to a technological showdown between AR and immersive VR technologies is something that cannot be predicted. In the past, this has occurred for example, with the videotape and DVD industry often with some innovations eventually losing out to the competition. The passage of immersive technology has been slow but there is significant investment and the general use of this technology is increasing all of the time. It seems unlikely that the AR offerings will immediately overtake the immersive market, immediately, if indeed they do, and perhaps each will have its place and niche to fill.

As regards Virternity, the goal of a compound or mixed reality is certainly going to be achievable in the foreseeable future. The challenge facing Virternity is not whether the technology will be there to fulfil the aims it has set for its particular brand of reality but the best way of utilising that technology to bring them to fruition. It might be suspected that this will be an evolving process and Virternity developers will need to be flexible and responsive in this regard. Appealing to a diverse user base who are likely to be using different platforms to experience VR is also another challenge. What Virternity faces is not the question of can it be done or how, but more to the point what is the best way of doing it to ensure the success of the Virternity universe.

Bibliography

Best Branded Google VR Cardboards. (2017). *Best Branded Google VR Cardboards*. https://www.viarbox.com/single-post/2017/01/20/Virtual-Reality-HMDs-2016-Sales-Numbers

Brewster, S. (2017). *Despite their hyped debut, virtual-reality headsets had sluggish sales in 2016. MIT Technology Review.* https://www.technologyreview.com/s/603208/behind-the-numbers-of-virtual-realitys-sluggish-debut/

Ewalt, D. (2016). Disruption Machine. *Forbes*, 76-86.

Gelernter, D. (1992). *Mirror worlds or the day software puts of the universe in a shoebox* (1st ed.). New York: Oxford University Press.

Noor, A. (2016). The HoloLens Revolution. *Mechanical Engineering*, 30-36.

Perry, T. (2017). Augmented reality: forget the glasses. *IEEE Spectrum, 54*(1), 36-39. doi:10.1109/mspec.2017.7802744

Raymundo, O. (2016). Tim Cook: Augmented reality will be an essential part of your daily life, like the iPhone. *IOS Central.*

Ricci, A., Piunti, M., Tummolini, L., & Castelfranchi, C. (2015). The Mirror World: Preparing for Mixed-Reality Living. *IEEE Pervasive Computing, 14*(2), 60-63. http://dx.doi.org/10.1109/mprv.2015.44

Rubin, P. (2017). *Facebook's Bizarre VR App Is Exactly Why Zuck Bought Oculus. Wired.com.* https://www.wired.com/2017/04/facebook-spaces-vr-for-your-friends/

CHAPTER SEVEN

Virternity: The Virtual Office

David Evans Bailey

This chapter discusses further the proposal of the Virternity project to provide virtual offices for those who wish to work at remote locations or even set up businesses that run in the Virternity world.

As far back as the late 1990's Virtual Offices were being proposed. The concept was then referred to as telecommuting. The employee would use the facilities of their office remotely and log into the systems provided by their company. They would be able to be contacted by phone as needed or by email. With the advent of the internet and now VR, the paradigm has changed. What is currently thought of as a virtual office and what it will be in a VR world such as Virternity bears examination. Traditional concepts of a virtual office as noted consist of access to office systems by remote login. The remote worker's machine becomes a terminal which acts as if it is part of the company's network systems and uses software such as Citrix Receiver to accomplish this. This type of arrangement is still commonly used for remote access to systems by companies or otherwise often by way of remote access using a web browser. A 2003 study comparing the traditional, virtual and home office concluded *"the results of this study indicate that telework offers the potential for enabling employees to better balance work and family life while at the same time enhancing business performance. The present study finds little evidence that telework has any negative business ramifications at all."* It goes on to indicate the obvious cost savings in not having to pay for office premises which contribute to a good business case. There is a note of caution made regarding a virtual office which indicates that work/life balance and family can suffer under these conditions unless it is carefully monitored. (Hill, Ferris, & Märtinson, 2003. p. 236). The study is not very specific about what a virtual office actually consists of, defining it as being able to work anywhere suitable without necessarily being designated as teleworking. In the context of Virternity the parameters are likely to be more fixed because of the limitations of current VR technology but this may well change with new advances. With current immersive products, it is probable that at least physically a VR worker will be based in a location, perhaps their home, and enter the VR immersive environment from there. As immersive technology becomes more mobile the operating basis will change again for this medium. In any case, the potential for someone to be at the office twenty-four hours a day continues to be an issue that must be managed. This will not be new to Virternity. Even in 1998, the work/life balance was being called into question with respect to the virtual office. This earlier research work noted *"Another important implication of this study is that virtual office teleworkers must learn how to disengage themselves from work."* and continued that training for office workers in how to manage their virtual working life was recommended. (Hill, Miller, Weiner, & Colihan, 1998, p. 681). However, in 2017 the virtual office model is well advanced along with and also due to the ability to access mobile networks with a plethora of devices that can be used to stay connected with the workplace and colleagues. Consequently, the workplace is entirely mobile for some. The circumstances that were foreseen in 1998 have come to fruition almost forty years later. One of the most recent studies by Messenger (2016) indicates that the evolution of new ICT (Information and Communication Technology) devices such as smartphones was something not predicted but that these have had a significant impact on the virtual office *"There was something important that Alvin Toffler could not foresee in his visionary book The Third Wave: The Internet and its effect on the use of ICTs. Toffler saw all work places of the information society relocated from the employer's premises to employees' homes."* (Messenger & Gschwind, 2016, p. 199). It notes also *"New ICTs enabled the mobile virtual connection of workers. As with the previous generations, it is precisely this technological advancement that triggered the further evolution of Telework."* (Messenger & Gschwind, 2016, p. 200). The advent of the smartphone has been a particularly momentous 'game changer' in terms of mobility. Applications that can allow the user to access information from anywhere coupled with the mobility provided by means of the mobile phone network is the element that has perhaps actually decoupled workers from the specific environs of a designated office space or their home. It opened the possibility of being able to carry out a job of work that is computer based from almost anywhere with the right equipment. The mobile network has arguably done more for mobility than any other single networking advance in the last two decades. As Messenger's paper concludes *"New ICTs, such as smartphones and tablet computers, have revolutionised everyday work and life in the 21st Century. On the one hand, they enable us to constantly connect with friends and family as well as with work colleagues and supervisors; on the other hand, paid work becomes increasingly intrusive into the time and space normally reserved for personal life. Crucial to this development is the detachment of work from traditional office spaces."* (Messenger & Gschwind, 2016, p. 205). Will VR and immersion change this even further? It is a fair question and currently, there are many unknown factors which have been discussed in other chapters including VR technology, applications and the investment in hardware and software for these platforms. The secondary issue being when will these be made available to the general public? Overall, however, the concept of immersive VR proposes to create not only a virtual office *per se* but an entirely new space in which to work albeit one that is virtual. This is not just a matter of moving the location of the office itself. It is inventing entirely new locations which are built and operated by software; the worker will be operating within a virtually created 3D environment. Virternity simply needs to provide the means to create such spaces and software applications that will facilitate it. The idea is not an entirely new invention and is already within the realms of possibility with applications under development. As an aside, it is possible to imagine this as a financial investment or as a way of financing the Virternity enterprise. The selling or renting of virtual real estate could be an attractive proposition.

In a piece for PC Magazine, editor Eric Grevstad writes *"According to GlobalWorkplaceAnalytics.com, regular work-at-home (among telecommuters, not self-employed individuals) has grown 103 percent since 2005, and 6.5 percent in 2014...This means that 3.7 million employees (2.5 percent of the workforce) now work from home at least half of the time."*

(Grevstad, 2016). This sizeable number endorses the shift in focus in terms of work location, although he also notes that the home is the still the most popular choice as a different office location. Improvements in productivity and job satisfaction have also been stated as benefits of this style of working. Home is certainly one of the places where many people might feel most comfortable and perhaps enjoying less stress in terms of commuting and office politics may be other factors in making this attractive. The virtue of a VR environment would seem to be that many factors within it can be easily changed. Customisable features within the VR office would enable a user to make it more 'homely' and more personalised. It is notable that in any office most employees tend to individualise their workspace and so VR is just a logical extension of that without any real cost implications to the business. Given that, as Grevstad says, Millenials are demanding a better work/life balance than perhaps their predecessors, it could be argued that this new generation is more likely to embrace the idea of the VR office more easily. (Grevstad, 2016).

Writing for the *Journal of Accountancy*, Jeff Drew, examined three companies who have closed their physical offices. One of the most significant tests of a virtual office, he writes, is this *"The biggest challenge with the virtual office is establishing and maintaining a sense of camaraderie among employees who rarely are in the same building, much less the same room."* (Drew, 2013, p. 27). This social aspect is often an important part of office life and the isolation from other co-workers will be a problem to some. Translating this to a VR environment would mean that the social interaction could be returned to the equation. VR would potentially remove that element of remoteness that might be felt from home working. Interaction under the currently accepted ways of remote working is usually limited to phone and Skype types of applications, as well as chats or email. The video Skype call is one way of giving more of a visual form of involvement with others and the incorporation of Skype for Business within Microsoft's Office suite has increased the availability of this kind of platform for internal and external corporate video communication. One of the next logical steps will be VR. There must be some caveats however in the sense that communication alone would perhaps not be sufficient for a virtual office application. Logically the use of an immersive headset would preclude being able to access the usual software accoutrements of an office such as email, word processing, the Internet, for example. A user would have to be able to operate almost entirely within the VR environment or at the very least a mixed reality environment and the launch of effective AR technology has yet to happen.

To balance this concern, a cursory examination of the field reveals that there are already several offerings in terms of VR office space or software which are either available or in development. *Breakroom* purports to be a virtual space where a user can park multiple virtual screens in a VR spaces which link into their Windows desktop. ("Breakroom", 2017). It is not entirely clear how this will operate in terms of the user being able to type information onto a keyboard if they wanted to use a spreadsheet for example. Jon Martindale describes another product called *Space* in Digital Trends *"When viewed through a VR headset, these panels can be moved, changed in size, shape and distance from your face, and they don't use up any more resources than they would if they were displayed on standard monitors, we're told."* (Martindale, 2016). *Space* will apparently utilise the camera facility on the HTC Vive, for example, to allow the user to see the keyboard and mouse thus turning an immersive environment into something that is also partially augmented. A similar blended reality style approach with multiple VR screens is being mooted by *LightVR* as described in an article for *UploadVR*. (Jagneux, 2016). These products so far are easy in concept but perhaps constrained in use by the technology and it is already possible to see the pitfalls inherent in a system which requires the use of a keyboard and mouse to become useful for desk based office work or any similar occupation requiring where the user needs to type. Aaron Frank says this in his article describing a virtual office experience for *Motherboard "As I put on the headset, I was taken to a space-world (though I could have opted for a cityscape) where web browsers and spreadsheets were suspended in air around me. The only thing keeping me somewhat tethered to the physical room was a camera pointed at the keyboard, which projected a video feed of my hands typing into my display."* (Frank, 2016). Quoting Larry Rosen, a

Professor from California State University, he notes that Rosen's concerns about the virtual office are that it would, in fact, be no different from the real world and that it might have too many distractions. Frank, however, described his own experience of the virtual office as 'awesome'.

In summary, it is clear from research that overall the virtual office is not only becoming more prevalent but can carry significant advantages over the normal office environment. The technology is also available to facilitate this, at least currently in the immersive arena. Applications are already being developed for VR-based virtual offices, though the state of this market is not entirely clear at this point in time. What this indicates for Virternity is that the means already exist to provide the VR office spaces in line with the project's aims. Because of the corporate element, this also has a potential for being a revenue stream. The challenge for Virternity is to produce an attractive enough offering at the right price and with the right functionality to bring that business and enterprise into their virtual world. As a result of this innovation, the Virternity enterprise may even profit from it.

Bibliography

Breakroom. (2017). We make breakroom. Retrieved 10 March 2017, from http://murevr.com/#about

Drew, J. (2013). How to open new doors by closing your office. *Journal Of Accountancy*, 24-29.

Frank, A. (2016). *I Worked in a VR Office, and It Was Actually Awesome - Motherboard. Motherboard.* Retrieved 10 March 2017, from https://motherboard.vice.com/en_us/article/i -worked-in-a-vr-office-and-it-was-actually- awesome

Grevstad, E. (2016). All signs point to telecommuting. *PC Magazine.*

Hill, E., Miller, B., Weiner, S., & Colihan, J. (1998). INFLUENCES OF THE VIRTUAL OFFICE ON ASPECTS OF WORK AND WORK/LIFE BALANCE. *Personnel Psychology*, *51*(3), 667-683. http://dx.doi.org/10.1111/j.1744-6570.1998.tb00256.x

Hill, E., Ferris, M., & Märtinson, V. (2003). Does it matter where you work? A comparison of how three work venues (traditional office, virtual office, and home office) influence aspects of work and personal/family life. *Journal Of Vocational Behavior*, *63*(2), 220-241. http://dx.doi.org/10.1016/s0001-8791(03)00042-3

Jagneux, D. (2016). *'LightVR' Wants You To Create Your Own Virtual Office Space. UploadVR.* Retrieved 10 March 2017, from https://uploadvr.com/lightvr-personalized-virtual-office-space-desktop/

Martindale, J. (2016). *Compute from the beach (or Mars) with Space, a VR office environment. Digital Trends.* Retrieved 10 March 2017, from http://www.digitaltrends.com/virtual-reality/space-virtual-reality-office/

Messenger, J. & Gschwind, L. (2016). Three generations of Telework: New ICTs and the (R)evolution from Home Office to Virtual Office. *New Technology, Work And Employment, 31*(3), 195-208. http://dx.doi.org/10.1111/ntwe.12073

CHAPTER EIGHT

Virternity: Transfer and storage of human memory into the Virternity environment and Shared memory (and experience) experimenting

David Evans Bailey

This chapter discusses further the proposal of the Virternity project to implement the digitised memories of people that are generated by sensor devices used in immersive, compound or mixed realities and share or 'relive' those experiences whilst in the Virternity world. The Virternity project moots this as an opportunity for personal gain without the associated risk.

There are two different ways that one could upload personal memories to virtual space. The first is often known as 'Transhumanism' or 'mind uploading' where the contents of an individual's mind are essentially meant to be copied and stored as computer code thus making it accessible to others, and even potentially becoming a cybernetic or virtual form of that individual. This method will be discussed in detail in a later chapter. The second is the uploading of personal experience gained using recording on devices capable of rendering a virtual copy and that is the subject of this discussion.

In order for another person to experience a virtual memory, it must first be recorded in a form which will allow it to then be viewed as immersive content. Recording devices capable of effecting this are available, as are the immersive devices on the market able to view the content. There are considerations in relation to this which should be of note. The prevalence of this type of content is of interest as might also be the psychological effects of viewing content in VR which might be deemed as distressing, violent or otherwise. Some analogies could be drawn to studies made on viewing such content in the medium of film or television. An allied question to this would be whether checks and balances should be applied in the Virternity space regarding the type of content available. The production of created experiences is also the subject of studies which can show whether these influence individuals viewing them in a way which is beneficial or otherwise. Virternity needs to consider these issues as part of its overall scheme.

One of the companies at the cutting edge of experience based VR is *8i* from New Zealand, for whom writer Sophia Stuart claims in an article for *PC Magazine* that *"It recently released a high-profile VR digitization of Matrix Academy, an educational tool for hairdressers, for L'Oréal. The company trained more than 2 million hairdressers globally in 2015, but with the new VR tool, student numbers can increase exponentially."* (Stuart, 2017). *8i* uses a rig designed from forty 'Point Grey' cameras to create volumetric holograms of people that can be placed in a VR setting. Sophia confirms that the simulation seems very real having tried it using an HTC Vive and concludes that this would make an excellent training tool. This is an example of high-end technology requiring software to digitise and produce the experience. Whilst this is laudable it is out of the frame of reference of most ordinary people wanting to share their memories in a world such as Virternity. The primary issue for most general contributors will be the recording and potentially editing technology that facilitates this. The implication is that they will be making a real life recording rather than a software based simulation such as that offered by *8i* and other similar enterprises. The number of 360 cameras at affordable prices is growing and this can only be set to continue as technology improves and progresses. These cameras must either be linked to a smartphone or are recording devices in their own right. (Vazharov & Vazharov, 2017). It is evident that correct placement of the camera to give a first-person perspective would be crucial. YouTube statistics reveal that over 300 hours of video are uploaded each minute. ("STATS | YouTube Company Statistics - Statistic Brain", 2017). The majority of this upload volume would be conventional video currently but 360 content is likely to increase across platforms such as YouTube and Facebook. This indicates that the concept of experience video is already very much part of the modern idiom which will help considerably to facilitate Virternity's venture into this area. There is also the ability to record experiences made in VR itself for replay at a later date, this could be likened to the plethora of gaming videos that exist on YouTube and are immensely popular.

The idea of being able to put yourself into the shoes of another using VR is being explored by a project called 'The Machine to be another'. This ongoing project uses real-time immersive feeds between two people to enable each of them to see the world from the other's viewpoint. The system works in the following way *"The system combines elements of telepresence and performance to generate the psychophysical experience of being present in the body of another. The user's movements are coupled to those of the performer through head-mounted displays, head tracking, headphones, microphone and servo controlled cameras. The performer follows user's movements in an identical space."* (Bertrand, Gonzalez-Franco, Cherene, & Pointeau, n.d.). This is a carefully controlled environment where users act in tandem with each other but assume the embodiment of the other person through the immersive process.

Although this is an art project, the results so far from a number of 'performances' show that empathy can be increased between different groups and also points to other applications such as psychotherapy and empathy research where this could be used. For Virternity this illustrates the potential value of such immersive or VR encounters beyond simple aims such as thrill seeking.

Why an experiential memory would be effective at all upon another is a function of immersion and VR. Immersive VR relies upon the concept of 'presence'. To explain this, it is simple enough to turn to an experiment which has devolved into a *de facto* test and demonstration of immersive technology and VR which is colloquially described as *The Virtual Pit* and which produces the following usual reaction *"Looking over the edge of the pit, nearly all visitors experience anxiety"* (Bailenson & Blascovich, 2011, p. 38). This is a virtual simulation which consists of a plank that appears to the participant to span a deep drop that ends on the floor of the room below. The viewer wears an immersive headset and whilst viewing this simulation is required to navigate the plank across an apparent virtual void. It is common for participants to experience anxiety and this manifests itself in such physical signs as toe curling and sweating palms with individuals often shaking their heads and refusing to attempt the experiment at all. This extreme experience, however, indicates how real the experience of VR can be. Presence is something Jeremy Bailenson who has been involved in VR research for many decades at Stanford University most succinctly defined in a lecture in 2013 as *"feeling like you are in the virtual world and forgetting that you are in the physical world"* (Bailenson & Gurley, 2013, 4:43). What he described is a psychological transition that would almost feel as if the person had been teleported into a different space. Viewing either a 360 video or a VR simulation will give the same effect and it is not the element of realism that seems to particularly regulate this as much as the presence of the person in the VR environment.

In reference to presence and as a case study it is worth mentioning that in terms of experiential content web providers in the sex industry such as *Pornhub* have been investing heavily in VR. Statistics for this site for 2016 illustrate that 38 million VR related searches were performed during that year an increase of 302% from the start of 2016. Allied with the factor of presence, the in-room first person perspective of such content is very likely to increase its appeal. ("2016 VR Porn Statistics Say VR Is Hot", 2017). This simply shows that the subject of human sexuality is an area which will continue not only to move its paradigm with the technology but be undiminished in consuming people's attention. Whilst this is not an area that Virternity has particular focus, it is at least a 'marker' which indicates that using VR to put oneself inside an experience is attractive to many people.

An examination of the potential effects of experiential VR material upon the viewer is also important. A study by *Eyewitness Media Hub* looked at the specific example of reporters having to view distressing footage being prepared for news outlets. Although it is not actually VR, the element of presence is undoubtedly there in terms of first hand viewing of such events on screen. It was notable from the research that *"40 percent of survey respondents said that viewing distressing eyewitness media has had a negative impact on their personal lives... Professionals have, for example, developed a negative view of the world, feel isolated, experience flashbacks, nightmares and stress related medical conditions... Repeated, cumulative exposure to traumatic eyewitness media was cited by many respondents as being particularly difficult professionally and increasing the feeling of vicarious trauma."* (Dubberley, Griffin, & Mert Bal, n.d.). The presence element of immersive VR has shown to increase affective responses in the viewer over screen based VR content. (Estupinan, Rebelo, Noriega, Ferreira, & Duarte, 2013). Based on this data and the above research it is perhaps safe to assume that distressing content viewed in an immersive scenario would increase the reaction of the viewer to that content, also known as vicarious trauma. Repeated exposure to such content could be detrimental to the viewer as the study shows. Additionally, a recent study which examined media violence exposure and children concluded *"We found an association between media violence exposure and physical aggression in children with multivariable adjustment for sociodemographics, home and neighborhood violence, and child mental health symptoms. This association was present and independent for media violence exposure in each of the 3 types of media examined (TV, video games, and music). Effect sizes increased with increasing time spent consuming video games and music."* (Coker et al., 2015). These findings are echoed in other similar types of study (Zheng & Zhang, 2016) but a more recent paper concludes that the studies in this area are inconsistent (Ferguson & Beresin, 2017). What can be said is that Virternity should consider the inclusion of some form of guidelines and policies regarding experiential content. These matters are bound to arise as they have for other sites such as Facebook and YouTube, where the problems of regulating graphic, violent and other similar content is an ongoing issue. As noted in a recent article in the *Chicago Tribune*, Facebook announced it would make decisions on whether to keep or delete graphically violent content depending on the intention of the video to condemn or raise awareness or whether it was just simply to glorify it. The article goes on to note that *"Now Facebook has, against its intentions, become the host for interventions into larger conversations about what sort of violence we should be seeing and discussing, and how to interpret those moments."* (Ohlheiser, 2017).

In summary, there is no technical barrier to the shared memory aims of Virternity. It is after all just another form of content and if anything, the storage requirements for such content would be of more concern. There is also no doubt that content of this nature would be attractive to the vicarious wanting to experience the memories of another. The number of reality TV shows that are prevalent is a testament to an enduring interest in other people's lives. The biggest issue for Virternity is likely to arise in the form of regulation or guidance for those posting content to be shared and re-experienced. The team must consider these aspects carefully and also include the legal implications of matters that may arise such as potential claims of psychological harm caused by viewing the same. In this respect, it is a matter to be approached with care, but nevertheless, represents an opportunity to many who will contribute to the Virternity shared experience.

Bibliography

2016 VR Porn Statistics Say VR Is Hot. (2017). *VRCircle*. Retrieved 13 March 2017, from https://www.vrcircle.com/2016-vr-porn-statistics-say-vr-is-hot/

8i. (2017). *8i.* Retrieved 12 March 2017, from https://8i.com/

Bailenson, J., & Blascovich, J. (2011). Infinite Reality: Avatars, Eternal Life, New Worlds, and the Dawn of the Virtual Revolution. HarperCollins e-books.

Bailenson, J., & Gurley, G. (2013). Infinite Reality.

Bertrand, P., Gonzalez-Franco, D., Cherene, C., & Pointeau, A. 'The Machine to Be Another': embodiment performance to promote empathy among individuals.

Coker, T., Elliott, M., Schwebel, D., Windle, M., Toomey, S., & Tortolero, S. et al. (2015). Media Violence Exposure and Physical Aggression in Fifth-Grade Children. *Academic Pediatrics*, *15*(1), 82-88. http://dx.doi.org/10.1016/j.acap.2014.09.008

Dubberley, S., Griffin, E., & Mert Bal, H. *Making Secondary Trauma a Primary Issue: A Study of Eyewitness Media and Vicarious Trauma on the Digital Frontline. Eyewitnessmediahub.com.* from http://eyewitnessmediahub.com/research/vicarious-trauma

Estupinan, S., Rebelo, F., Noriega, P., Ferreira, C., & Duarte, E. (2013). Can Virtual Reality Increase Emotional Responses (Arousal and Valence)? A Pilot Study. *Lecture Notes In Computer Science 8518:541-549 · January 2013.*

Ferguson, C. & Beresin, E. (2017). Social science's curious war with pop culture and how it was lost: The media violence debate and the risks it holds for social science. *Preventive Medicine, 99,* 69-76. http://dx.doi.org/10.1016/j.ypmed.2017.02.009

Ohlheiser, A. (2017). *Facebook Live wants to give people a voice, but it's mostly noticed for violence. chicagotribune.com.* from http://www.chicagotribune.com/bluesky/technology/ct-facebook-live-violence-wp-bsi-20170108-story.html

Stuart, S. (2017). How VR Holograms Can Train Everyone From Hairdressers to Astronauts. *PC Magazine.*

STATS | YouTube Company Statistics - Statistic Brain. (2017). *Statistic Brain.* Retrieved 12 March 2017, from http://www.statisticbrain.com/youtube-statistics/

The Machine to be Another. (2017). *The Machine to be Another.* from http://www.themachinetobeanother.org/

Vazharov, S. & Vazharov, S. (2017). *The Best 360-Degree Cameras for Capturing Your Surroundings. Best Products.* from http://www.bestproducts.com/tech/gadgets/news/g1752/360-degree-cameras/

Zheng, J. & Zhang, Q. (2016). Priming effect of computer game violence on children's aggression levels. *Social Behavior And Personality: An International Journal, 44*(10), 1747-1759. http://dx.doi.org/10.2224/sbp.2016.44.10.1747

CHAPTER NINE

Virternity: Forecast system based on neural network and blockchain Virternity connections

David Evans Bailey

This chapter discusses further the proposal of the Virternity project to enable and augment forecasting and prediction using the Virternity space. Virternity conjectures the idea that neural networks combined with blockchain will allow them to conduct precise multivariate analysis of possible courses of events. Thus, intimating that reliable forecasts and foresights will be introduced into everyday life. This could be a possible way of looking into the future with better certainty in their opinion. They also submit that the system will be able to track in real-time mode the state of a person's health and even offer advice and future options.

It is useful to first understand the thinking behind this idea. Blockchain is a system which indelibly writes transactions that link information together and cannot afterwards be erased. Initially focused on financial virtual currencies, the blockchain technique has wider applications that can encompass many types of transactions. Imagine the scenario where even though a person might have deleted posts or comments from their social media these are still available in the system. The implication is that this type of information and opinion can be used for forecasting trends or possible future events. The concept of personal future forecasting implies an expert system that may present outcomes based upon an individual's current courses of actions, beliefs or opinions, among other things. The mining of health information implies connection with a tracking device that provides this information and consults a health, expert system, which can give advice based on its database and algorithms.

In the preface of his book on neural networks computer scientist Huajin Tang defines them in the following way; *"Artificial neural networks, or simply called neural networks, refer to the various mathematical models of human brain functions such as perception, computation and memory. It is a fascinating scientific challenge of our time to understand how the human brain works. Modelling neural networks facilitates us in investigating the information processing occurred in brain in a mathematical or computational manner."* (Tang, & Hanneghan, 2015). Tang notes that neural networks are the pathway to intelligent machines. The computer model that mimics brain activity should be capable of recreating the decision and intelligence of the brain also. He indicates that the current focus is on *Recurrent* networks which allow information to flow in multiple directions rather as neural cells operate as opposed to *Feed Forward* networks which pass information in one direction forward. Neural networks also involve complex mathematics. Research continues in this field as another paper on Neural Networks and Genetic Programming concludes *"This paper described an evolutionary algorithm for neural network design with the self-configuration technique. The algorithm allows us to find compact and accurate structure of neural networks model, while the self-configuration technique permits the exclusion of a human expert from the process of setting parameters."* (Loseva, Lipinsky, & Kuklina, 2015, p. 689). The algorithms contained in the type of neural network of this study are self-configurable and as such can learn and adapt to forecasts without intervention. In the Virternity space evidently forecasting of future events perhaps based upon historical data will be of interest, or even in the case of What-If scenarios to aid decision making and planning. Virternity envisages something more than just an expert system but rather an artificially intelligent system that gleans information from many sources.

It must be pointed out that there are privacy and other implications which would arise from the idea of reading other people's data. Whilst 'big data' and 'data mining' are the new buzzwords of this decade not all social opinions posted online can be relied upon. The notable failure of election forecasting in the recent American presidential race is an example of where this has not worked. Political Science researcher Mark Huberty discusses this issue in a paper on social media forecasting. He writes that *"our experience to date in forecasting important events, political or otherwise, has not always borne out the promise of new predictive powers. Success in predicting what people will want to buy, or what ads they might click on, has not translated into reliable predictions in sectors such as public health or finance."* He also indicates that research by online opinion polls has also shown them to be vulnerable to systematic bias. (Huberty, 2015, p. 992). Evidently, the mining of data which examines what people look at online does not necessarily translate into political opinion and in particular where political views are concerned it would appear that online activity and even opinion does not necessarily reflect voting patterns. He notes some factors that make social media unreliable for forecasting of critical or important events: an unstable and dynamically changing user base, what is important to people online and offline may be completely different, people change the way they operate online according to their desire to get noticed and rule changes by providers. In other words, the supposition that people are necessarily being honest online could be a fallacious one at best. He concludes *"The assumption of a relatively stable link between online and offline behaviour appears to work reasonably well when forecasting purchasing behaviours, estimating advertising effectiveness, or identifying potential contacts. Beyond those cases, it appears to be less reliable."* (Huberty, 2015, p. 1005). The hopes of forecasters prior to these failures was very much pinned upon the idea of virtual social media communities providing an accurate litmus test to views across many different arenas including those of politics. The reality of these forecasting attempts is that they did not reflect the actual polling results at the ballot box. This is a matter of concern to forecasting organisations going forward if the data that is mined is not reliable and cannot be used in a meaningful way to make predictions. For a prediction to be accurate, the data upon which it is based must also be an honest reflection of events or opinions or else the result will be incorrect at best. This issue will no doubt be reflected in the virtual world of Virternity. At this point, what kind of data will be available for attempted forecasts is not clear and cannot be conjectured until the actuality of Virternity comes into being. This remains, therefore, an open issue to be further explored once the data is available upon which forecasting models can be used in the Virternity space, at that point the accuracy of the data and the predictions can be more readily assessed.

With respect to the other part of this proposition, the prospect of tracking and monitoring personal health is not necessarily a new idea. Wearable devices which monitor heart rate, for example, and track steps and exercise are readily available linking to a variety of applications to allow users to track their own results. Proposals for online monitoring systems for health are ongoing as for example noted in this conference paper from two healthcare researchers *"We propose the use of an open and publicly accessible online social media platform (OSMP) as a key component for ubiquitous and personal remote health monitoring."* Their study compares various offerings in the then market place with respect to health monitoring using wearable devices and by smartphone. (Khorakhun, & Bhatti, 2014, p. 287). They suggest that social media platforms such as Google+ and Facebook could be used as vehicles for this type of monitoring providing that privacy issues are addressed in terms of who can access the data and for what purpose. A platform such as Virternity would face the same issues if healthcare monitoring was introduced into that virtual world. A Chinese study recently investigated attitudes to wearable devices and found that consumers had a 'fair to good' opinion of these. There was also optimism amongst those surveyed that the devices would improve and become more useful. The inability to use them properly or analyse the data were cited as reasons to stop wearing them. (Wen, Zhang, & Lei, 2017, p. 136). This is a positive outlook for what might be considered by some to be invasive devices sharing private information. There are more invasive implanted devices that are used for cardiac monitoring which however do provide valuable early warning signs of heart and health problems and have a high rate of patient acceptance (Varma, & Ricci, 2015). Remote healthcare and e-health is part of ongoing initiatives in countries which contain remote and rural areas such as Australia enabling a better level of healthcare for the residents of these districts (Banbury, Roots, & Nancarrow, 2014). There is certainly already a precedent for health monitoring which Virternity could take forward without too much resistance. Data protection and security would obviously need to be of paramount concern, as would the presentation of results that are worthwhile or of use to the individual. If an expert system could give guidance based upon health data, then this would be more beneficial and likely to receive a positive response. Additionally, health professionals would seem to welcome the idea of being able to monitor the health of individuals at risk more closely. Overall this part of the initiative is both laudable and achievable as regards the Virternity space.

Bibliography

Banbury, A., Roots, A., & Nancarrow, S. (2014). Rapid review of applications of e-health and remote monitoring for rural residents. *Australian Journal Of Rural Health*, *22*(5), 211-222. http://dx.doi.org/10.1111/ajr.12127

Huberty, M. (2015). Can we vote with our tweet? On the perennial difficulty of election forecasting with social media. *International Journal Of Forecasting*, *31*(3), 992-1007. http://dx.doi.org/10.1016/j.ijforecast.2014.08.005

Khorakhun, C., & Bhatti, S. (2014). Using Online
Social Media Platforms for Ubiquitous,
Personal Health Monitoring. In *2014 IEEE
16th International Conference on e-Health
Networking, Applications and Services
(Healthcom* (pp. 287-292).

Loseva, E., Lipinsky, L., & Kuklina, A. (2015).
Eensembles of neural networks with
application of multi-objective self-configuring
genetic programming in forecasting problems.
In *2015 11th International Conference on
Natural Computation (ICNC) Natural
Computation (ICNC.*

Tang, H., Tan, K., & Yi, Z. (2007). *Neural networks*
(1st ed.). Berlin: Springer.

VARMA, N., & RICCI, R. (2015). Impact of Remote
Monitoring on Clinical Outcomes. *Journal Of
Cardiovascular Electrophysiology, 26*(12),
1388-1395. http://dx.doi.org/10.1111/jce.12829

Wen, D., Zhang, X., & Lei, J. (2017). Consumers'
perceived attitudes to wearable devices in
health monitoring in China: A survey study.
*Computer Methods And Programs In
Biomedicine, 140*, 131-137.
http://dx.doi.org/10.1016/j.cmpb.2016.12.009

CHAPTER TEN

Virternity: Experiments with a deep immersion into the Virternity space (long-term existence only in the virtual part of the Virternity space)

David Evans Bailey

This chapter discusses further the proposal of the Virternity project to implement experiments which will see volunteers living solely through the medium of mixed reality via Virternity space. According to their proposal, the participants are intended to live isolated from their physical existence and contact their friends and family solely through immersive and semi-immersive VR. Their lives, appearance, work, leisure and all other aspects will be undertaken through

Virternity itself. The stated aim of these experiments is to enable Virternity developers to obtain data which could lead to the digitisation of human consciousness.

It is important to examine if there is any precedent for this proposal which considers the idea of removing individuals from the trappings of their physical existence and replacing it with a virtual existence and what those studies might reveal. To date, there have been few documented experiments which explore long term exposure in immersive VR. One VR ethics researcher Micheal Madary points out in his paper on the topic ethical conduct for VR *"First, and perhaps most obviously, we simply do not know the psychological impact of long-term immersion. So far, scientific research using VR has involved only brief periods of immersion, typically on the order of minutes rather than hours. Once the technology is adopted for personal use, there will be no limits on the time users choose to spend immersed."* He also identifies several potential risks associated with this such as: addiction, manipulation of agency, unnoticed psychological change, mental illness, and lack of what is sometimes vaguely called "authenticity" (Madary, &

Metzinger, 2016, p. 13). His supposition is correct in that the widespread use of immersive VR already removes any element of regulated use other than as a matter of personal choice. Overall the study by Madary indicates not only that caution needs to be exercised but that more research in this area needs to be done. Careful research adhering to suggested ethical guidelines are recommended by Madary which should exclude certain vulnerable groups, such as children. The paper cites a number other issues such as behaviour manipulation, privacy and neglect of others which could potentially be associated with long term immersion. The short answer at this point is that the impact of long term immersion is not known. In conjunction with this another research paper voices multiple concerns regarding the convergence of social networks and VR in which the authors delineate a number of detailed threats to privacy with the advent of virtual reality social networks. These mostly centre around the vulnerability of data in VR, the loss of anonymity and privacy. They suggest that participation in VR is effectively a license to allow surveillance and even recording of activities. They conclude *"The threats to privacy are well known and serious; whilst those to autonomy are less-well known but equally as profound. Moreover, it is suggested that the threats to privacy themselves may in fact constitute a threat to autonomy, as people might become used to a life under surveillance."* (O'Brolcháin et al., 2015, p. 26). They suggest more research is devised which will develop appropriate ethical responses to these concerns. It is evident that as an individual subsumes themselves into such a virtual environment as Virternity issues of individual protection, which are taken for granted in the physical world due to legal constraints, will arise and more consequently because of the way that the technology can enable privacy invasion in multiple ways. It is to a large degree down to the provider of the environment, such as Virternity, to address these issues. The technology itself *de facto* already exists that would allow surveillance and recording of everything an individual does within VR. Long term immersion becomes not just an issue of physical concern but one of individual rights and protections that need to be regarded.

In one of the first documented short studies, researchers Steinicke and Bruder exposed a single participant to 24 hours of immersion in 2014. The participant spent 11 two hour blocks in a purposely set up physical room which mirrored the virtual room he was exposed to. No communication outside of VR was allowed and bathroom breaks were incorporated into the breaks between VR sessions. The Oculus HMD had to be worn at all times during the VR periods even during periods of sleep. Results from this research in particular indicated simulator sickness arose whilst moving around the room, changes to accommodation distance for the eyes and most significantly *"Place and Plausibility illusion: Several times during the experiment the participant was confused about being in the VE or in the real world, and mixed certain artifacts and events between both worlds."* (Steinicke, & Bruder, 2014, p. 4). Postural disequilibrium is noted in a paper by another researcher Lackner, noting disruption also following a return to physical world orientation. (Lackner, & DiZio, 2014). The disorientation graph in Steinicke's study is of concern since this became increasingly higher as the experiment progressed indicating more disorientation correlating with a longer time spent in immersion. With Virternity contemplating long term exposure to this kind of environment due attention would obviously need to be given to the physical needs but also to the potential for confusion within the minds of the subjects taking part. At what point, would virtuality and physical reality cross over and become effectively the same thing to a person? Virternity researchers and developers would be advised to pay due cognizance to concerns that are raised with regard to not only personal welfare of participants in long term immersion experiments but the impact of the same in all aspects of their lives, including their privacy and in the wider context how this will impact on widespread immersive participation which is the Virternity's ultimate goal.

Parallels can be drawn with other studies of prolonged isolation and immersion outside of VR. One such study is the Mars 500 project by NASA. The project simulated a Mars Mission with a crew inhabiting an environment which corresponded to a Mars spaceflight including the journey to and from Mars as well as an orbited mission around Mars itself. The six crew members were subjected to the same conditions that the mission would impose including communication delays as the spacecraft's distance from Earth increased. Interpersonal communication and socio metrics were tested. Among other findings the study concluded that *"In the course of extended stay in the hermetic chamber, the human subjects experience social frustration and crowding, facilitating both negative and positive experience as well as anxiety, related to these factors...Under isolation conditions people are faced with dialectical contradiction between the desire for privacy/personal space and affiliation, which is expressed in social penetration, such as an openness and an expressiveness."* (Tafforin, Vinokhodova, Chekalina, & Gushin, 2015, p. 27). Whilst the parameters of the test are different, the elements of divorcing the participants from their normal physical environs and customs and placing them into a situation of prolonged close association of another environment has similarities with immersion in VR. There will inevitably be isolating factors in VR simply by virtue of having to contact the normal environment and others through immersive or semi-immersive hardware. This in itself will isolate an individual to a degree and, it must be conjectured, they will also have no contact with other individuals through the physical environment that would be their habitual mode of living. The issue of privacy may be one which concerns participants in the sense that privacy in VR is itself an open question at this point. It may drive more open and expressive behaviour in VR as suggested above. Unknown factors remain at this time, such as the state of technology at the point that these experiments will be undertaken. This is pertinent not only in terms of immersive or augmented reality devices but also because developments in haptics will continue to change the sensory paradigm of VR.

The psychological effects of exposure to immersive environments have been the subject of much study. Jeremy Bailenson at Stanford University has lead research into this area since the 1990's. As a leading expert in this field Bailenson's studies are relevant to potential issues arising from long term immersion. In one relevant piece of research which was a study into embodiment and sexualisation, he concluded *"this study has demonstrated that women can be affected negatively by the avatars they wear. Women may be at risk for experiencing self-objectification and developing greater rape myth acceptance, and these attitudes may influence their behaviors both on and offline."* (Fox, Bailenson, & Tricase, 2013). This is of note since it indicates that exposure in VR and the appearance of the individual's avatar can have a negative affect psychologically which can then go on to cause changes in their behaviour. That is simply one aspect of VR influence among many which highlight how an individual will react psychologically to what they encounter in an immersive environment. In another study, Bailenson examined the ability to influence environmental concerns in subjects exposed to these issues in an immersive environment. He concluded that VR could be a tool for persuasion and modification of towards positive behaviours and that further research was needed in this direction. The persistence of behavioural changes following exposure to the interactive virtual environment was noted in marked difference to persuasive arguments on paper or by video. (Ahn, Bailenson, & Park, 2014). Other studies by Bailenson have noted the effects of height differences, skin colour differences and a variety of other factors which can be persuasive to an individual in VR. (Blascovich, & Bailenson, 2011). Awareness of these types of manipulating factors is important to participants who are going to spend long periods of immersion within VR. These types of findings also have a high level of significance to Virternity in terms of the likely psychological effect of prolonged exposure to a virtual immersive type of environment on an individual. It would suggest that the virtual environment would elicit the same reactions to situations that are found in the physical world and in this sense the participant is likely to accept the VR experience as real. Having noted that point, then these types of studies also support the idea that living in the virtual world for long periods would be possible, at least in the psychological sense. Making the conscious experience of the individual in Virternity become a real experience would be something that was within the realm of possibility to be accomplished. These proposed experiments of long term immersion in the Virternity environment are certainly technologically possible even now and will become ever more so as developments in this arena continue. The challenge is not so much in the hardware as the shaping of these experiments to take account and mitigate the factors mentioned. The management of the issues surrounding the people involved rather than the technology that facilitates it will continue to be of primary concern.

Bibliography

Ahn, S., Bailenson, J., & Park, D. (2014). Short- and long-term effects of embodied experiences in immersive virtual environments on environmental locus of control and behavior. *Computers In Human Behavior, 39*, 235-245. http://dx.doi.org/10.1016/j.chb.2014.07.025

Blascovich, J., & Bailenson, J. (2011). *Infinite reality.* New York: William Morrow.

Fox, J., Bailenson, J., & Tricase, L. (2013). The embodiment of sexualized virtual selves: The Proteus effect and experiences of self-objectification via avatars. *Computers In Human Behavior, 29*(3), 930-938. http://dx.doi.org/10.1016/j.chb.2012.12.027

Lackner, J., & DiZio, P. (2014). Virtual environments and the cyberadaptaion syndrome.

Madary, M., & Metzinger, T. (2016). Recommendations for Good Scientific Practice and the Consumers of VR-Technology. *Frontiers In Robotics And AI, 3.* http://dx.doi.org/10.3389/frobt.2016.00003

O'Brolcháin, F., Jacquemard, T., Monaghan, D., O'Connor, N., Novitzky, P., & Gordijn, B. (2015). The Convergence of Virtual Reality and Social Networks: Threats to Privacy and Autonomy. *Science And Engineering Ethics, 22*(1), 1-29. http://dx.doi.org/10.1007/s11948-014-9621-1

Steinicke, F., & Bruder, G. (2014). A Self-Experimentation Report about Long-Term Use of Fully-Immersive Technology.

Tafforin, C., Vinokhodova, A., Chekalina, A., & Gushin, V. (2015). Correlation of etho-social and psycho-social data from "Mars-500" interplanetary simulation. *Acta Astronautica*, *111*, 19-28. http://dx.doi.org/10.1016/j.actaastro.2015.02.005

CHAPTER ELEVEN

Virternity: Copying the human consciousness and memory to the Virternity space (experiments with digital copies of real persons)

David Evans Bailey

This chapter discusses further the proposal of the Virternity project to engage in serious experiments that will lead to the emergence in the virtual space of 'digital copies' or what the project terms as 'people-originals'. The project designers intend that the experiments will make it possible to protect the original people from harm at this early stage. The intention is to continue the experiments until a person can be fully transferred into the Virternity space.

The idea of connecting the human mind in some way with digital technology is particularly contained in the various concepts of Transhumanism. These range from connecting or augmenting the body and the mind using computer-based devices to a complete 'mind upload' into digital space. A brief examination of this field was made in chapter one and this chapter will examine the issues and claims in more detail. Whether the human mind or consciousness can indeed be uploaded to a computer is currently a matter of debate and not a factual reality since the ability to do so has not yet been demonstrated. Much of the debate centres and will continue to centre around discussion as to whether the entirety of the consciousness of a human and their memories is held in a physical organ such as the brain or whether they are not. This is a philosophical question as much as it is also scientifically debated since there has been no irrefutable proof of this either way although there has been much conjecture. Were the human consciousness and memory to be an entirely physical structure then the matter of finding a way to upload this to another physical structure such as a computer may be difficult but not impossible to ultimately achieve. If, however, this assumption was not so then the possibility of achieving it multiplies in complexity.

To date, there has been no successful transfer of human memory to a machine although there are proposed methods of doing so. The Virternity project is right to state that this is an experimental stage because it is certainly no more than that at this time. The issue of whether in engaging in a copy of the memories the person will not be harmed is also a matter for deliberation. A proposed process for mind uploading has been described in detail by proponent and neurologist Ken Hayworth (2012), its technique hinges around Focused Ion Beam Scanning Electron Microscopy (FIBSEM) which is used to trace nerve processes in small slices of brain tissue. At the time of writing, he noted that the process has a limitation of sample size. However, he claims to have overcome this with samples 20 microns thick and proposes that this could be used to section and scan an entire human brain. He makes this assertion based upon these assumptions "*A central thesis of this paper is that an electron microscope volume image of an entire chemically-fixed and plastic-embedded human brain (with sufficient resolution to allow the tracing of synaptic connections between all neurons) would contain sufficient information to fully encode the unique memories, skills, and personality of that particular individual.*" The premise upon which this is based relies heavily upon the idea that human consciousness is indivisible from the physical structure and thus contained within it. Hayworth continues to discuss the idea that once a scan of the brain had been effected in this way it could be transferred into computer code. He hypothesises that this code, though a simulation, would exhibit first person conscious experiences that are like those experienced by the original individual from which they came. (Hayworth, 2012, pp. 88-89). The hypothesis itself also relies upon research which shows that Artificial Intelligence (AI) studies can produce models of the human cognitive architecture. The argument of whether this would be a simulation or the entire consciousness of the person is in one degree philosophical and in the other hard to prove at this moment without empirical data or evidence. There are other issues which surround the invasive nature of the technique proposed as noted here *"Electron imaging of brain tissue also requires that this tissue be structurally stabilized by removing all water from within the tissue and infiltrating every nook and cranny of extracellular and intracellular space with a curable plastic resin."* Not the least of these is the lack of machinery and techniques to carry out the sectioning required of a whole human brain in order to scan it. (Hayworth, 2012, p. 98). Hayworth lays out in detail how this could be achieved and the designs for the machinery that would be required. He concludes that the investment in this technology would be justified by subsequent experiments following the first successful scanning of a human brain. From a Virternity standpoint, this technique does not fulfil the stated aim of preserving participants in the experiment from harm. In order to effect the brain scanning transfer that Hayworth proposes would require the mortality of the individual in the physical sense, since their brain has to be removed and sectioned thus rendering it subsequently unusable and unable to support life. Such extreme measures may, however, be potentially incompatible with the initial aims of Virternity.

A less invasive technique might be that of continuous recording of memories of an individual from a given point. A recent research paper suggests this to be a way of modelling the cognitive faculties of a human and that by developing what it terms deep neural networks simulations could actually learn from these recorded experiences (Lee et al., 2017). Another field involves the use of a mind-machine interface. Current research into these kinds of interfaces involve the use of equipment which allow the user to control artificial devices such as limbs through their brainwaves or via implanted electrodes in brain or spinal tissue. A recent study of the advancement of such an interface for spinal cord injury patients indicates that positive research has been underway in this area for some time albeit in controlled laboratory settings and has focussed upon neurons in the motor cortex since the drive is to restore motor functions by controlling artificial or robotic appendages. (Hawryluk, & Guan, 2016). However, devices that can read and decode brain signals are perhaps a far less invasive form of mind transfer. Another study cites the use of an Electroencephalogram (EEG) device known as a 'NeuroSky Mind Wave Sensor' which senses brain waves produced during eye blinks to interpret commands to control a wireless mobile robot. (Stephygraph, Arunkumar, & Venkatraman, 2015). A further research paper discusses successful experiments involving monkeys using a Brain Machine Interface (BMI) to enable the monkeys to manipulate computerised screen based interactions by brain waves. (Ahn, 2016). The indications that research into brain interfaces is progressing is supported in this statement by researcher Farhad Shir *"it appears that the trend in the future of the HCI devices and systems is moving toward providing systems and devices that could efficiently convey the brain signals to command gadgets, while a user is thinking about commanding the gadgets."* (Shir, 2015, p. 11). As his paper also reflects, research is very much slanted towards mobility at this time. That is not to say that if brain waves can be interpreted for motor control that other areas such as memory could not also be available to this kind of scanning device. Indeed, a paper proposing a new branch of investigation called 'Cognetics' which marries robotics with bodily awareness indicates this about memory *"With regard to memory, new wearable haptic devices might also be used to record and subsequently re-experience haptic events, as is possible for vision and audition through cameras/projectors and microphones/loud speakers, respectively."* (Rognini, & Blanke, 2016, p. 163). The authors propose that haptic and other devices will record what happens around and to a person so that they can be re-experienced. This might be implied as mind uploading by proxy through devices other than the brain itself but where the resulting feedback could be experienced by the senses of another. Overall it can be concluded from these types of study that whilst such indirect and less invasive technology does not yet exist for 'mind uploading' ongoing research in this area is very likely to produce new breakthroughs in this field sooner rather than later.

It seems certain that some form of, at least, memory transfer to computer from a human will be possible. Whether this consists of a conscious personality or not is going to be a matter of some controversy as well as empirical investigation. Artificial intelligence itself may produce the simulation of a conscious, self-aware thinking mind which would test the definitions of what it is to be human or indeed to be 'alive'. Technology and philosophy researcher John Sullins challenges the Transhumanist view of the world *"At least since the writings of Descartes, the role of the human body in cognition had been the subject of philosophical and psychological discussion. Traditional AI researchers somehow missed the philosophical and psychological works of Dewey, James, Heidegger, Wittgenstein, Merleau-Ponty and others and instead built a research program whose foundations rested on the shifting sands of the mind-body problem. It was not their interest to study the mind as a property of human bodies, but rather to see it as a formal system that could be implemented on a computer."* He continues asserting that Transhumanists reject the notion that identity and the human body are not indivisible. (Sullins, 2000, p. 16). Many philosophers such as Descartes see the mind as immaterial and as such able to transcend the physical world. If this was to be true, then the ability to capture the consciousness of a person and place it in a machine might be difficult if not impossible to envisage. Sullins asserts through his study of the work of philosophers that the identity would degrade once severed from the body which contains it, he contends that the body cannot be transcended and hence the goal of Transhumanism is not one that can be accomplished. Equally there are supporters and strong proponents of Transhumanist theories, researcher Loredana Terec-Vlad and in a recent paper she asserts *"We believe that the possibility of achieving eternal life will not remain a goal, whereas through the new technologies and artificial intelligence we will have the chance to live in a virtual reality, in a future possible world"* mitigating her assertion only as speculative theories but noting that these appear on the priority lists of a number of researchers. (Terec-Vlad, 2015, p. 122). Terec-Vlad concludes with her support and personal belief that a technological singularity within some context will be possible such as through a downloaded consciousness operating through artificial intelligence. In another paper, however, Terec-Vlad explores the bio-ethics and religious concepts of Transhumanist aims and concludes that these are violated by the goals of science in this regard. Dichotomies of this nature fuel the dispute between the schools of thought. (Terec-Vlad, 2015, p. 39).

The argument around mind-uploading technology will continue, it encompasses not only the question of consciousness but the ethical and moral dilemmas that it engenders alongside these. Until a method exists to actually facilitate the upload of the human mind in part or in whole to virtual reality it will remain a matter to be contested. Once a method does exist then other issues will inevitably arise that will need to be addressed. For Virternity there is no conflict in terms whether the aims of the project can be met. The stated aims may be achievable in the future and the probability is high that human minds can be uploaded in whole or part to a machine. How one might then define this new 'personality' is not something that can currently be addressed. It is also clear that some invasive techniques for uploading that are being mooted and investigated would destroy the human counterpart in the process. It can only be recommended that if Virternity wishes to retain the goal of keeping subjects from harm then these are not techniques that should be contemplated in the first instance. These ultimate aims of Virternity in no way detract from the things that can already be accomplished using immersive, mixed or augmented realities which can connect humanity to the Virternity world without the need to upload the person in the process.

Bibliography

Ahn, S. (2016). Becoming a network beyond boundaries: Brain-Machine Interfaces (BMIs) as the actor-networks after the internet of things. *Technology In Society*, *47*, 49-59. http://dx.doi.org/10.1016/j.techsoc.2016.08.003

Hawryluk, G., & Guan, J. (2016). Advancements in the mind-machine interface: towards re-establishment of direct cortical control of limb movement in spinal cord injury. *Neural Regeneration Research*, *11*(7), 1060. http://dx.doi.org/10.4103/1673-5374.187026

Hayworth, K. (2012). ELECTRON IMAGING TECHNOLOGY FOR WHOLE BRAIN NEURAL CIRCUIT MAPPING. *International Journal Of Machine Consciousness*, *04*(01), 87-108. http://dx.doi.org/10.1142/s1793843012400057

Lee, S., Lee, C., Kwak, D., Ha, J., Kim, J., & Zhang, B. (2017). Dual-memory neural networks for modeling cognitive activities of humans via wearable sensors. *Neural Networks*.

http://dx.doi.org/10.1016/j.neunet.2017.02.00
8

Rognini, G., & Blanke, O. (2016). Cognetics: Robotic
Interfaces for the Conscious Mind. *Trends In
Cognitive Sciences*, *20*(3), 162-164.
http://dx.doi.org/10.1016/j.tics.2015.12.002

Shir, F. (2015). Mind-Reading System - A Cutting-
Edge Technology. *International Journal Of
Advanced Computer Science And Applications*,
6(7).
http://dx.doi.org/10.14569/ijacsa.2015.06070
2

Stephygraph, L., Arunkumar, N., & Venkatraman, V.
(2015). Wireless Mobile Robot Control through
Human Machine Interface using Brain Signals.

Sullins, J. (2000). Transcending the meat: immersive
technologies and computer mediated bodies.
*Journal Of Experimental & Theoretical
Artificial Intelligence*, *12*(1), 13-22.
http://dx.doi.org/10.1080/095281300146281

Terec-Vlad, L. (2015). From Divine Transcendence to
the Artificial One. Challenges of the New
Technologies. *Postmodern Openings*, *06*(01),
119-129.
http://dx.doi.org/10.18662/po/2015.0601.08

Terec-Vlad, L. (2015). What about Eternal Life? A
Transhumanist Perspective. *Postmodern
Openings*, *6*(2), 33-41.
http://dx.doi.org/10.18662/po/2015.0602.03

CHAPTER TWELVE

Virternity: Elaboration of legal, psychological and financial issues of the existence of virtual persons

David Evans Bailey

This chapter discusses further the proposal of the Virternity project regarding legal measures that might be required within the virtual space of Virternity. Virternity also envisages that new business and social services will be available to seniors and that new issues will be raised in this regard and new solutions required: ranging from petty offences merged into the digital reality and ending with psychological and philosophical implications of new features and abilities, new experiences and ways of life. The Virternity project considers the idea that the technological, legal and psycho-physiological basis will be established with respect to the virtual space within the first generation of people anticipating that they would have already spent the full life in the compound reality. It may then be within the realm of possibility for those individuals to move entirely into the virtual world.

Popular culture is already paving the way for the acceptance of a mixed reality existence with fictional television series such as *Westworld* (Wood et al., 2016). These types of dramas unwittingly or not create an atmosphere of possibilities within society, and the ongoing launch of immersive and other types of VR technology is also widely known. Understanding that Science Fiction becomes Science fact will usher in an era of more practical concerns for most. If an existence which includes VR becomes a practical proposition then the normal issues of society such as legality, criminality and so forth also enter the province of this new way of living. Legal expert and professor Joshua Fairfield examines this issue in an article on the subject and points out the anomalies between physical law and virtual law *"The growing application of online law to realspace is a problem because offline and online law have significantly diverged. Consider the simple act of purchasing a book. If you purchase a book offline, you own the book. If you purchase an e-book, you own nothing."* (Fairfield, 2012, p. 59). Fairfield's point is whether new laws governing online events such as the idea of ownership should apply or whether offline and existing statutes should be able to cover these situations. He reasons that there is a danger that courts will judge these new situations without considering existing legislation and he proposes that basing mixed reality laws using analogies to similar situations in the physical world would resolve many issues that might arise. He also notes that at the time of writing there was a lack of legislation addressing mixed reality situations. Another problem he raises is the definition of mixed reality in the sense that it must be precise based upon what it does and doesn't do. The fact of placing a table, for example, in mixed reality means that it can exist in the physical world by virtue of its projection there through technology. An action that might occur as a result of that table being virtually in the physical space could have legal consequences if say a person leant upon the table in a restaurant and fell over because the table wasn't really there. He asserts that accuracy is vital in legal definition. (Fairfield, 2012, p. 68). His article attempts to define the terminology of each type of reality precisely and is an excellent point of reference. He notes that there is a breadth of academic legal literature that covers virtual reality and the development of 'common law' in these types of environments but then he also indicates a lack of literature with respect to mixed reality environments where legal cross over issues could occur, citing a case where a person hit by a car whilst following Google Maps on a mobile phone subsequently failed in the courts. (Fairfield, 2012, p. 78). He concludes somewhat profoundly on this point *"All virtual worlds are to some extent mixed: they are experienced by real world people, who interject elements of reality into the virtual world. The world may be virtual, but the economic, artistic, and even romantic lives of the participants are quite real."* (Fairfield, 2012, p. 84). This is a concept that could often be overlooked for the fact that there might be a tendency to separate the idea of the virtual existence from that of the physical existence. In a mixed reality situation, such as that proposed by Virternity these two existences merge and it must not be forgotten that behind the avatar is a real conscious being with all the trappings of life, other desires and accoutrements that this entails. Fairfield makes excellent arguments which correlate well with the intentions and beliefs of the Virternity project. Virternity propounds exactly the idea that for the participants or even 'inhabitants' of their virtual world the experiences in which they participate will certainly be real to them. Assuming that in the future people are conducting some part of their daily existence within such an environment, then a legal framework is certainly required just as it exists within the physical world.

Law and Digital Media Scholar Nicholas Suzor provides a detailed examination of the role and rule of law in virtual communities in his treatise which indicates that utopian based ideas of autonomous legal frameworks for virtual worlds could be in many ways a flawed argument. He asserts that the very fact that virtual communities are a captive market built on considerable financial investment and bound by their own tight and complex legal agreements, which are difficult for the average participant to understand or depart from, easily indicates that vested interests will most often prevail over common interests of participants. He says that *"legitimate self-governance is an extremely difficult ongoing process. Theorists have demonstrated that of the four modalities of regulation identified by Lessig (code, law, the market, and social norms), none are value neutral, and none can be relied upon to provide Utopian results."* (Suzor, 2010, pp. 1825-1830). In essence, although self-governance is desirable it appears that virtual world providers may weight their own regulations in their own favour rather than a balanced view that separate a justice system and legal framework would provide. He sounds a different note of caution regarding intervention which illustrates the example where state interventions that have been detrimental to virtual communities which then tends to delegitimize state intervention as a policy. There may be circumstances where state intervention is desirable for the benefit of the individual. As for example, the use of Supreme Courts in many countries setting and revoking legal precedent. There is a further danger that he outlines where private laws made in virtual communities become enforceable by actual world courts *"In looking at virtual communities experientially to see both how they are different from real spaces and how they are the same, one of the striking realizations is that limitations on the exercise of power are conspicuously absent. Thus, as the use of virtual communities grows in importance in all aspects of a citizen's life, the public law of the state is slowly replaced by the private "law" of the provider."* Thus, he notes that in this type of instance the legal framework of the virtual community may override constitutional rights that are enshrined in actual physical law. The erosion of constitutional rights would naturally be of detriment to the individuals who are part of that virtual community albeit that this might benefit the providers. This outlines the dichotomy between self-governance and state governance where neither extreme is necessarily beneficial to the parties involved. (Suzor, 2010, p. 1835). His concerns are that virtual providers can have absolute discretion over the lives of virtual participants even up to the possibility of summary eviction and arbitrary judgements over their existence. Western democratic legal frameworks are rooted in the prevention of abuse of absolute public power and constitutionally framed in order to provide limitations to this. Suzor details several strands of the rule of law which provide safeguards for the individual against the state and which are unlikely to be present in the legal frameworks of virtual communities. He says *"If law is not merely restrictive or wholly subject to the interests of the powerful, but can and does play a useful role in restraining the raw exercise of power, then reducing the role of law poses a risk in that power within virtual communities is not subject to the rule of law"* (Suzor, 2010, p. 1837). Suzor's article overall is a comprehensive treatise on the subject of the rule of law and how it should be, could be and has been applied to virtual communities and is recommended reading for anyone contemplating the legal minefield that is virtual space. His conclusion cites this overarching principle *"The values of the rule of law and the rights of citizens are continuously protected by the evolution of the private common law. The myriad legal determinations regarding how power can be exercised by members of society substantially construct the rights and interests of all citizens."* (Suzor, 2010, p. 1886). He reinforces the traditional concepts upon which common law is founded and the values which have taken centuries to develop in democratised societies. Virtual spaces are still in their infancy and although this treatise was written over 17 years ago, the issues and principles delineated are very much of current and future concern. As he discussed in his paper, social spaces such as Facebook have already encountered the boundaries between imposed terms and conditions and those of the 'real' world. Because virtual networks span several countries and laws in those countries may differ this is also of concern. Homophobia, as an example, is an issue where differing levels of discrimination and non-discrimination some of which are protected by statute leave individuals without recourse if the rule of law of one country over another was applied to them in virtual space. This also raises issues of legality and geographical jurisdiction which are among the many areas that developers of the Virternity project must address in terms of governance.

As well as legal frameworks for VR, there is a matter of ethics and codes of conduct that should be considered for participants and world creators regardless of whether these are subsequently preserved with actionable legality. In his book *Being Really Virtual*, researcher Frank Steinicke discusses the matter of ethics in virtual space and notes that Madary and Metzinger (2016) suggested three particular overriding rules for VR usage based loosely upon Asimov's Robotic Laws (1977). The first rule: Humans (as well as animals) must not be seriously harmed due to VR. The second: Avatars must not be seriously harmed; except for cases in which Rule #1 would be violated. The third: Immersion must not be concealed. (Steinicke, 2016, pp. 150/152). These are good starting points to encompass and examine actions which may cause harm or conceal the fact of immersion from an individual. Naturally, an examination of what is defined as harm, both physical and psychological would need to ensue and following from this laws could be put into place. However, it must be said that these ethical principles fall very short of a constitutional statement or declaration of rights that would seem necessary for a world that aims to become a substitute or at least a significant other to the physical existence of human beings. Virternity presents an opportunity to shape a new virtual existence with far reaching ambitions. The rights of citizens within that burgeoning digital existence should be of primary concern. Establishing not only a fair and just system of jurisprudence is a necessary step in protecting those rights. Virternity would do well to consider the constitutions and systems of the most successful democracies as a frame of reference. Without this framework, the only recourse open to an individual to contest legal issues will be the justice systems and courts of various states through which Virternity may operate or where participants may physically reside. Much academic research and work exists in regard to the legal issues around virtual spaces for reference material. Virternity's challenge is to support their stated aims with a just administration and governance of their world.

Bibliography

Asimov, I. (1977). *I, robot* (1st ed.). New York: Ballantine Books.

Fairfield, J. (2012). MIXED REALITY: HOW THE LAWS OF VIRTUAL WORLDS GOVERN EVERYDAY LIFE. *BERKELEY TECHNOLOGY LAW JOURNAL, 27*(55), 54-84.

Madary, M., & Metzinger, T. (2016). Recommendations for Good Scientific Practice and the Consumers of VR-Technology. *Frontiers In Robotics And AI, 3.* http://dx.doi.org/10.3389/frobt.2016.00003

Steinicke, F. (2016). *Being Really Virtual* (1st ed.). Cham: Springer International Publishing.

Suzor, N. (2010). THE ROLE OF THE RULE OF LAW IN VIRTUAL COMMUNITIES. *BERKELEY TECHNOLOGY LAW JOURNAL, 25*, 1817-1885.

Wood, E., Wright, J., Harris, E., Mind, T., Clavier, T., & L'Oeil, T. (2016). *Westworld (TV Series 2016–). IMDb.* from http://www.imdb.com/title/tt0475784/

CHAPTER THIRTEEN

Virternity: Unlinkable payments (Untraceable Transactions) implementation

David Evans Bailey

This chapter discusses further the proposal of the Virternity project regarding the idea of making blockchain transactions untraceable in the Virternity space. Virternity asserts that some users may prefer not to leave information about their private life in the digital space and that the project should respect privacy and individual freedoms. They imply that they will provide a new feature allows a user to make payments with untraceable origins around the world.

Are blockchain transactions capable of being untraceable currently? In an article for Governance

Directions consultant, Tess Hoser notes "A blockchain is transparent, with each participant having a complete and traceable record of all transactions on the blockchain." (Hoser, 2016, p. 609). The implication is that even though blockchain users are provided with an encoded key when using a blockchain system, the participant could potentially be identified by tracing that key back to them as the initiator, although this is unlikely to be available other than to system administrators for that blockchain system and relies on a centralised register which is not always the case. Harvard Professor Marco Iansiti also confirms what Hoser says in his article The Truth about Blockchain where he points out that users have a choice to remain anonymous or reveal their identity which is linked to unique 30 plus character code which identifies them and their transactions (Iansiti, & Lakhani, 2017, p. 125). There must be some tangible link in place, nevertheless, for a participant to be able to return to view their transactions at some later time. The issue still remains as to whether this 30 plus character code can be ultimately linked back to them. In many cases, particularly those of public blockchain networks this link resides in the digital wallet of the transaction holder, rather than a central register. There is a risk to the wallet holder of losing access to the wallet or even losing the wallet itself. Security of the wallet often becomes the responsibility of the wallet holder unless it is obtained through a wallet provider and held on a server.

Founder of Bitcoin Satoshi Nakamoto writes in his proposal for Bitcoin as a peer to peer cash system that the level of privacy achieved by bitcoin using blockchain would be greater than the traditional banking system since no third party holds the details of the participants and transactions. By virtue of using the keys then the individuals concerned remain anonymous to outside viewing. He goes even further to suggest that owners of transactions may have multiple identifiers to prevent mining of the data and finding out bitcoin holdings of individuals by aggregation using unique ids. In this scenario, the owner would not be identified but their holding and number of transactions would be. (Nakamoto, n.d., p. 6). In an almost ironic twist, it is also known that Satoshi Nakamoto is a pseudonym and that the real individual behind Bitcoin remains anonymous. Obviously, the transaction keys are held somewhere and for Bitcoin, this usually is a digital wallet. However, it may be that private bitcoin networks will provide an investors database which creates a more fault-tolerant way of ensuring transaction holder's details do not get lost even though on the other hand this could compromise their anonymity and vulnerability to hacking.

Security expert Allison Berke writing for the Harvard Business Review notes that "In the *bitcoin system, ownership is demonstrated through the use of a private key (a long number generated by an algorithm designed to provide a random and unique output) that is linked to a payment, and despite the value of these keys, like any data, they can be stolen or lost, just like cash. These thefts are not a failure of the security of bitcoin, but of personal security; the thefts are the result of storing a private key insecurely. Some estimates put the value of lost bitcoins at $950 million"* (Berke, 2017, p. 5). The implication, as noted above, is that the onus is most likely to be upon the user to retain the security of their digital key and that if this is somehow lost or even stolen then they can lose access to their assets or even have fraudulent transactions made on their behalf. This is certainly an issue which users would not want to experience, understandably. How the user can be protected against this is unclear, since systems like Bitcoin do not maintain a central register of keys, therefore, making the owner difficult to trace, but also making it very difficult to claim identity if their key itself is lost or stolen. Berke goes on to say that private blockchain providers must make decisions about lost keys particularly if these refer to physical assets. She asserts that with Bitcoin there is no recourse for lost keys and it is almost impossible to recover stolen transactions because they appear the same whether they originated from a legitimate node or otherwise (Berke, 2017, p. 5).

Faith in the security of a system is paramount for users dealing their own finances. Faith in traditional banking systems has been built up over many years. A recent article in *Euromoney* indicates that the banking sector itself is now moving towards pilot blockchain projects. A recent study of 75 banks, in fact, noted that 50% have invested in blockchain or will this year and the other half will do so by 2018. The aim is to facilitate settlements and payments at a faster rate and thus much of the development is interbank distributed networking aspiring to reduce the time money is transferred between accounts to seconds rather than days as it currently is internationally. (Lee, 2017). The same security issues that face individuals with blockchain will be less relevant on interbank transactions in the sense that bank security is already high. With centralised registers of fund owners and clients, the financial chain is traceable thus reducing the problem of fraud and other associated issues. The fact that banking institutions are entering the blockchain arena is an endorsement of the technology itself and potentially ultimately may provide competition to the efforts of private consortiums such as Virternity who wish to capture the market of their users within their own offering. The type of security problems outlined above which hinge around fraud and lost and stolen security keys are something which must be faced by Virternity developers and they will need to address them in order to attract long-term use of their system and also compete with more established institutions who may ultimately move into the blockchain arena more fully once they have gained experience with interbank transactions. Virternity may face a choice between providing digital wallets at the risk to the investor and participant or otherwise some form of centralised investment holding database may be the way forward with appropriate security measures in place to protect it.

Associate Professor and researcher Vincenzo Morabito makes a significant point in his book *Business Innovation through Blockchain* where he indicates particularly that private and public blockchain networks have important differences hinging mainly around the fact that participants in private blockchains are known to the provider and that participants in public blockchains are not. Where the participants are known in some way to the blockchain network a trust element is entered which is not present when participants are public and thus could be anybody. Since only permitted participants can read or write data and participate in transactions in private blockchain then it might be assumed that the potential for security issues might be thus curtailed. (Morabito, 2017, p. 9). Morabito also asserts the lack of trust on which the blockchain system is founded saying *"the blockchain is a distributed file system or a shared data structure built on the concepts of 'mistrust'. Its architecture provides a solution to the management of transaction files across multiple systems. A transaction ledger is created and propagated throughout the network and each participant has an exact copy of the ledger at all times. Participants do not need to know or trust each other."* (Morabito, 2017, p. 72). In other words, as opposed to a banking system which requires the bona fides of clients before they can become participants, the blockchain system has no such strictures and this is also something that is mooted as a benefit of these kinds of systems. Anonymity has its own set of issues which focus around the areas of potential criminality and money laundering, as an example, but in terms of what Virternity wishes to provide with untraceable transactions then blockchain does give them the means to do so. Morabito also discusses the concept of Proof of Work (PoW), the traditional way that bitcoin works versus Proof of Stake (PoS). PoW is a way of calculating transaction codes which prove that the work has been done by a legitimate participant, a hacker would, in theory, be unable to gain access to the correct codes in order to spoof this transaction code. However, on the downside according to Morabito, this method is expensive on computer resource. An alternative PoS depends upon the entities that hold a stake in the network itself and who will be contributing to the mining of coins *"we can say that the resource that the network security is dependent on is the ownership of the coin itself, which implies proof - of - ownership that is also scarce. For the authentication and reception of a transaction to occur (whether fees of transaction or new coins), some of the coin must be owned by a miner"* (Morabito, 2017, p. 11). He argues that PoS has more advantages of PoW but that it might allow a participant with a large stake in a cryptocurrency to dominate the market in some way, for example by influencing rates. He also notes that hybrids of the two schemes also exist which may provide the best of both worlds. Virternity will have to choose one of these schemes to implement its version of a digital currency and blockchain operated services. It may be that the PoS or hybrid system might be more attractive in terms of the security it offers.

There appears to be a preoccupation among blockchain developers to protect the integrity of their transaction system from hacking and interference as one of the top priorities. This is understandable since where financial transactions are at stake, the attraction for the criminal element is high. The duplication of blockchain transactions, faking and other forms of misappropriation are well thought out in terms of how they might occur and what must be put in place to prevent it. Due to the measures that blockchain providers have initiated in this regard the likelihood of a successful cyber-attack upon a system which is blockchain based seems of a lower order of magnitude. The issue of privacy is a different thing. Participants always need to be able to access their own transactions otherwise the preservation of their data is pointless. Every linking system will have a weak link and in this case, it will most likely be the point where the real user has to link with their coded pseudonym identifier that keeps them anonymous. How this part of the chain is protected is as important since that source point is otherwise to some degree vulnerable even if that degree constitutes an extremely small risk. Anonymity can be achieved by key coding and that is standard blockchain style practice. Untraceability relies upon others not being able to connect the dots to the real user behind the coded presence online. This is the challenge for Virternity, the project is capable of producing a well coded and protected system at the transaction level. The same invulnerability or even impregnability must also hold at the user level where it is needed in order to preserve anonymity and untraceability if that is what is desired by the participants involved.

Bibliography

Berke, A. (2017). How Safe Are Blockchains? It Depends. *Harvard Business Review*, 1-6.

Hoser, T. (2016). Blockchain basics, commercial impacts and governance challenges. *Governance Directions*, (Vol 68 Issue 10), 608-612.

Iansiti, M., & Lakhani, K. (2017). The Truth about Blockchain. *Harvard Business Review*.

Lee, P. (2017). Blockchain SHIFTS from theory to practice. *Euromoney*, 72-77.

Morabito, V. (2017). *Business innovation through blockchain* (1st ed.). Springer International Publishing.

Nakamoto, S. Bitcoin: A Peer-to-Peer Electronic Cash System.

CHAPTER FOURTEEN

Virternity: Communication channels development

David Evans Bailey

This chapter discusses further the proposal of the Virternity project regarding the idea of reducing the speed of blockchain messaging. The Virternity team claims to have found the key to virtually instant messaging. They assert that this will introduce to the world of digital communication the main blockchain advantages - the authenticity, integrity and reliability of information. The claims will be examined in as far as possible against known data.

The idea that blockchain can be used for instant messaging is not entirely a new concept. Online investigations reveal that at the time of writing there are initiatives already in progress in this direction. A new product known as *Echo,* a peer to peer instant messaging platform using secure blockchain technology to underpin it, bills itself as progressing towards an alpha release on Android. As noted in this article *"Echo aims to deliver a full-feature decentralized chatting app. It is everything you'd expect from a regular messenger: free and easy to use, but also secure, private and encrypted."* The CEO of *Echo,* Christoph Hering, indicates that the closest competitor to this is WeChat which is the largest social messenger provider in China. (Marshall, 2016). *Echo* plans to offer P2P worldwide encrypted chat services which will also include a wallet that will allow instantaneous money transfers all protected by blockchain technology. (Hering, 2017). *Echo* advertises itself as a completely secure in the cloud service which will run as a multi-currency system thus offering some of the functionality that is also being developed by the Virternity project. Virternity will be using their own cryptocurrency as part of the financial element within any money transfer, payment or messenger service. With respect to the instantaneous element of blockchain messaging, *Echo* is claiming to have also solved this problem with their own software in development and scheduled to launch sometime in 2017. Another entrant into this domain is DARPA (*Defense Advanced Research Projects Agency*) *who* an online article cites as seeking a secure messaging system for battlefield communications and office based defence messaging. The writer notes that *"DARPA envisions three stages for the project. The first would focus on the development of a system 'built on the framework of an existing blockchain framework',* *suggesting that an existing blockchain like bitcoin's could be used directly or as inspiration."* (Higgins, & Southurst, 2016). That DARPA is investing in blockchain technology is confirmed in a number of sources which includes the fact that a contract was signed in 2016 for $1.8 million with Galois and Guardtime Federal with the aim of researching the use of blockchain for securing critical defence systems. This level of interest and investment from an organisation for which security would seem an essential component to their operational capability is indicative of the confidence that blockchain technology has engendered in the wider community. (Warner, 2016). Overall these examples illustrate that blockchain techniques are permeating new areas of transaction based systems over and above online and cryptocurrencies and that these applications do indeed include instant messaging.

It would be useful to examine the level and type of use of Instant Messaging itself since that would be indicative of whether high investment in this area might be justified. A recent study of the use of Mobile Messaging in China found that users of messaging applications who felt an emotional attachment to these used them more. The study summarised it as this *"when consumers identify with the MIM applications, perceive congruence between their self-concept and MIM applications and perceive the beauty of MIM applications, they feel emotional attachment towards MIM applications."* It refers to the necessity to have the applications for instant messaging but at the same time emphasises the importance of the aesthetics of the application which factors combined make users functionally dependent upon them. The study also notes that the active use of such information systems, in general, is not a well-researched area. (Wu, Lu, Gong, & Gupta, 2017, pp. 156-163). The results from the study show that a high percentage of users have been active on messaging for more than 5 years and that they use their message application up to 10 times a day. Whilst this may be a small sample it indicates that messaging applications themselves seem to continue to be at the forefront of mobile applications. Another research project which investigated *Snapchat* particularly found that it was one of the top three messaging applications used by survey respondents and that they tended to use it for one to one conversations rather than in a group scenario. The study says that *"With IM, users can engage in more intimate and private conversations, allowing them to share their problems with communication partners more easily, and allowing for better intimacy and a sense of connection."* It goes on to assert that *Snapchat* allows for longer and more deep and meaningful conversations than perhaps a social networking site such as the Facebook wall would facilitate. It continues *"Our study highlights how Snapchat become effortlessly embedded within its users daily communication practices and is currently the most popular form of IM in par with SMS and Facebook Communicator."* Overall the research suggests that it appeals more to the younger demographic such as students and is almost a substitute for sharing moments that would otherwise be enjoyed when physically in each other's company. (Piwek, & Joinson, 2016, pp. 364-365). It is also useful to note that as early as 2011 a review of empirical research into instant messaging indicated that there were over a billion users worldwide and users sent an average of 53 messages per day. The review indicated that instant messaging is associated with online self-disclosure and increased intimacy with friends. (Fogel, 2011, pp. 13-17). These factors are of particular interest since not only is the high use of IM applications significant but that there is a tendency to discuss what might be considered essentially private matters would highlight the need for security of content. The psychology of why online chat facilities inspire such confidence in making personal disclosures is not necessarily relevant to this chapter and it is sufficient to simply know that this is an important factor of such channels of communication. Secure data transmission for Instant Messaging is not a new initiative and proposals for such architectures have been put forward before (Florez, Logreira, Munoz, & Vargas, 2016), (Del Pozo, & Iturralde, 2015). Knowing that the content of such chats can be somewhat sensitive then the protection of personal communication would be seen as paramount. As far back as 2005 instant messaging was viewed as a target for hackers and there is no indication that this has abated since (Leavitt, 2005). The proposals for secure messaging systems tend to be encryption based without the added element of blockchain that Virternity proposes to implement.

Instant messaging can be summarised as being a product and application that will continue to be in demand for the foreseeable future. The nature of instant messaging and its use seems to engender a situation where more intimacy is likely between parties engaging in chats online and also much of it is one to one and of a personal nature. It might also be seen as a substitute for face to face conversations conducted at a distance. Security of instant messaging must, therefore, be seen as a necessity. The use of blockchain as a secure mechanism for messaging applications is currently somewhat new and an area which is open to exploitation in terms of the limited number of competitive products using this technology. Overall Virternity is in a prime position to potentially take the lead in this market assuming that the speed with which they can bring a suitable product to fruition can capitalise on this momentary advantage. It is unlikely that the gap between competing products using blockchain for messaging will remain open for very long before others take up the challenge. All this notwithstanding, the wider issue of how instant messaging would work or be used in a VR style of environment is an area that has not been probed. This secondary issue will be more fully understood when VR immersive reality and mixed reality use is more prevalent and social communities in VR are more prevalent. It is likely that the way instant messaging works in this wise will develop over time. What is perhaps more important currently is to have the technology in place and take hold of the challenges that are presented now. This is perhaps where Virternity can certainly rise above the competition if they heed that old adage *carpe diem* and indeed do take the initiative to 'seize the day'.

Bibliography

Del Pozo, I., & Iturralde, M. (2015). CI: A New
    Encryption Mechanism for Instant Messaging
    in Mobile Devices. *Procedia Computer Science*,

63, 533-538.
http://dx.doi.org/10.1016/j.procs.2015.08.381

Florez, Z., Logreira, R., Munoz, M., & Vargas, J. (2016). Architecture of instant messaging systems for secure data transmision. *2016 IEEE International Carnahan Conference On Security Technology (ICCST)*. http://dx.doi.org/10.1109/ccst.2016.7815685

Fogel, J. (2011). INSTANT MESSAGING COMMUNICATION: SELF- DISCLOSURE, Del Pozo, I., & Iturralde, M. (2015). CI: A New Encryption Mechanism for Instant Messaging in Mobile Devices. *Procedia Computer Science*, *63*, 533-538. http://dx.doi.org/10.1016/j.procs.2015.08.381

Hering, C. (2017). *ECHO - Free Encrypted Private Chat + Instant Cloud Money Transfer. ECHO APP*. Retrieved 10 April 2017, from https://my-echo.com/

Higgins, S., & Southurst, J. (2016). *DARPA Seeks Blockchain Messaging System for Battlefield Use - CoinDesk. CoinDesk*. from http://www.coindesk.com/darpa-seeks-blockchain-messaging-system-for-battlefield-back-office-use/

INTIMACY, AND DISINHIBITION. *Journal Of Communications Research*, *2*(1), 13-19.

Leavitt, N. (2005). Instant messaging: a new target for hackers. *Computer*, *38*(7), 20-23. http://dx.doi.org/10.1109/mc.2005.234

Marshall, A. (2016). *Powered by Blockchain, New Decentralized Messenger to Save Data, Battery and Time. CoinTelegraph*. from https://cointelegraph.com/news/powered-by-blockchain-new-decentralized-messenger-to-save-data-battery-and-time

Piwek, L., & Joinson, A. (2016). "What do they snapchat about?" Patterns of use in time-limited instant messaging service. *Computers In Human Behavior, 54*, 358-367. http://dx.doi.org/10.1016/j.chb.2015.08.026

Warner, M. (2016). *DARPA Contract to Verify Blockchain Integrity Monitoring Awarded to Galois and Guardtime Federal | Chain-Finance.com. Blockchain-finance.com.* from http://blockchain-finance.com/2016/09/17/darpa-contract-to-verify-blockchain-integrity-monitoring-awarded-to-galois-and-guardtime-federal/

Wu, T., Lu, Y., Gong, X., & Gupta, S. (2017). A study of active usage of mobile instant messaging application. *Information Development, 33*(2), 153-168. http://dx.doi.org/10.1177/0266666916646814

CHAPTER FIFTEEN

Virternity: Universal Secure storage: research, inventions, pieces of art, etc.

David Evans Bailey

This chapter discusses further the proposal of the Virternity project regarding the idea of enabling a secure storage facility for valuable works. Virternity asserts that copyright protection is a long and expensive process of registration or publication. They point out that this renders work vulnerable to theft and registration by other individuals. They assert that some scientific innovations may be suppressed for commercial or political gain. Virternity proposes that they will provide a secure copyright database which will be immediately available dispensing with delays and costly registration. Right of authorship will thus be proven from the very moment of work is uploaded to Virternity storage. Virternity proposes the preservation of research results, invention, pieces of artistic culture for mankind, and additionally essential science can be shared, even anonymously if required, and without the intervention of vested interests. In essence, Virternity proposes to be an open published register of ownership and intellectual property rights. The Virternity project will provide a protected space that also allows access to materials by consent of the authors and originators.

The idea of using blockchain techniques to generate storage databases is in line with current thinking. Engineers and academics Asharaf and Adarsh write in a recent book about decentralised computing *"The Distributed public ledgers pave way for the backbone of Decentralized Internet of Things (IoT) and Internet of Everything by providing a reliable backend which can securely store everything coming to the Internet."* They discuss the idea that these ledgers will be facilitated by blockchain technology and focus mainly upon governments and corporations who might use it for repositories of important information such as the land registry, passports or tax records. (Asharaf, & Adarsh, 2017, p. 32). They claim that by using blockchain and what they term a 'consensus approach', whereby there is no reliance upon a third party for processing and storing the information, that not only costs but processing times will be drastically reduced. Their argument relies upon the immutable fact of blockchain transactions being non-erasable and thus a permanent record. To use their example of a passport application this would imply that confidential data and the history of the application would be traceable by the applicant and the issuing agency thus potentially reducing the opportunity for fraud and reducing the time from application to issue. The consensus strategy is explained thus *"With the consensus strategy, the Blockchain technology can effectively solve the concurrency problem in a completely distributed manner. Instead of having a central authority that maintains a database and guards its authenticity, a copy of the entire database is distributed to every node in the network. These nodes follow the consensus protocol and compare their versions together through a continuous process of 'voting'. The version that gets the most votes from the network is accepted as authentic, and the process repeats indefinitely."* (Asharaf, & Adarsh, 2017, p. 34). This illustrates the advantage of blockchain in that there are multiple copies of the same chain of information across a distributed network. A process of matching occurs which effectively authenticates repositories against each other. The algorithms validate their own database against the other databases on other nodes and ultimately achieve a consensus of valid data. Certainly, in theory, this seems workable and in practice is used by currencies such as Bitcoin to establish the validity of ledger updates and entries. The entries do not necessarily have to correspond to monetary values. What Asharaf and Adarsh are advocating could be summarised with their statement *"The Internet of Things (IoT), cloud and blockchain are three massive tech trends that could combine to create an entirely new method of data process known as IoT-based computation."* (Asharaf, & Adarsh, 2017, p. 34). In effect, Virternity is striving for a new way of storing and managing 'things' in a new virtual paradigm which they propose to create. The technologies that are now available will assist the Virternity project in these endeavours.

It is useful to examine whether any inroads have been made into computer based blockchain storage other than that of financial or currency based information. A website named *Proof of Existence* which advertises a document registration service requests potential clients to *"Use our service to anonymously and securely store an online distributed proof of existence for any document. Your documents are NOT stored in our database or in the bitcoin blockchain, so you don't have to worry about your data being accessed by others. All we store is a cryptographic digest of the file, linked to the time in which you submitted the document. In this way, you can later certify that the data existed at that time. This is the first online service allowing you to publicly prove that you have certain information without revealing the data or yourself"* ("Proof of Existence", 2017). This service appears to be based upon a similar idea to that of Virternity which is using blockchain technology in order to store a document and the information about its ownership. The website asserts that this will enable owners of copyrighted material to demonstrate their ownership of the same and furthermore with a timestamp verifying the time the material was registered and uploaded. In addition, the software will prevent further copies of the document being uploaded in an attempt to replace the original if there have been any changes or alternations to the document. Thus, attempts at fraud are reduced or even removed. The software uses the Bitcoin blockchain as its vehicle for embedding the information and creates an SHA256 digest in the bitcoin blockchain. This can be looked at as an early example of an open source platform which is piggybacked onto an existing blockchain network. The disadvantages are that it is run by a single individual and has no organisation to back it up, thus software maintenance and other such dependencies rest with that person as a single point of failure. However, it is an excellent proof of concept with respect to the ideas that Virternity wishes to implement showing that it not only can be done but that it already is being done.

As a further example Blockverify.io is a website which offers anti-counterfeiting capabilities. *"We believe in the potential of blockchain technology to improve anti-counterfeit measures in different industries and have a significant positive social impact"* ("Blockchain Based Anti-Counterfeit Solution", 2017). The service works by supplying a tag which is attached to the goods that a company wants to ensure are genuine. This tag is verifiable at any stage through the supply chain process with reference to the *Blockverify* database which uses blockchain to store the information about the product. The blockchain provides a transaction history for that product. The company asserts that it can help identify counterfeit or stolen goods as well as whether the product was diverted to a different location and also identify fraudulent transactions. Other similar services being advertised on the internet include *That's Mine*, a service which uses the bitcoin blockchain to identify ownership of things, *Ballotchain* for vote recording and *Insurechain* for insurance processes. ("Blockchain solutions for Automotive", 2017). Although it is unclear as to whether some of these products currently exist the intention to use blockchain for transactions that are unrelated to finance is clearly there. This is evidently a new area for blockchain technology given the few applications that currently exist. Virternity has an opportunity to take their ideas forward in this regard. One obvious point is that most application providers are not also implementing their own blockchain domains and are using existing providers such as Bitcoin. One drawback of doing this could be the fact that such blockchain systems are primarily set up to manage crypto style currencies and not primarily asset registration or other similar applications. They may not have space for all the necessary information and this means that to some degree existing blockchain systems may need to be slightly manipulated in order to make them work for these other types of requirements. Virternity has the potential to provide a more customised or perhaps flexible blockchain setup which will accommodate many different users and different applications. The fact that they are arriving later into the blockchain arena means that they may capitalise on the success of others and also benefit from solutions to any issues that older purveyors may have to have overcome in the process. This may perhaps put Virternity in a better position overall than some of their competitors in the blockchain field.

Associate Professor and researcher Vincenzo Morabito writes in Business Innovation through *Blockchain* that *"By using math and cryptography, blockchain provides an open decentralized database of any transaction involving value such as money, goods, property, work or even votes."* His comprehensive treatise on blockchain certainly endorses the idea that blockchain can extend into many areas beyond finance and into those already mentioned above that are being developed. He says that in the sense a transaction can be verified by the whole community means that blockchain is 'trustless' technology. He explains what he means *"in this case, 'trustless' means that the 'value' over a computer network can be verified, monitored and enforced without the need for a trusted third party or central institution."* This is the virtue of blockchain over centralised registration and to a large degree, the network distribution of the blockchain database gives a level of fault tolerance as there is no single point of failure. He summarises it this way *"the future economy will move towards one of distributed property and trust, where anyone with access to internet can get involved with blockchain based transactions. Blockchain technology can be thought of as wills and contracts that execute themselves. It will become a global decentralized source of trust."* (Morabito, 2017, p. 22). In his view blockchain readily facilitates the types of enterprise that Virternity wants to undertake. As a champion of blockchain technology, Morabito envisages many diverse uses for secure data storage and retrieval. The concerns regarding data integrity, the ability to delete or change data, are to a large extent mitigated by blockchain. The audit trail that blockchain provides, as well as a high level of security, does bode well for the idea of placing sensitive information into blockchain networks. Another blockchain expert writing for *Harvard Business Review*, Professor Michael Mainelli, notes that proof of identity is a perennial problem for people from all classes of society and demographics. Identification is key to ownership and property rights. He asserts that blockchain databases or registers are commonly owned because no third party actually owns them or maintains them *per se*, there is a mutual maintenance by data miners. The use of blockchain for identity tracking is certainly not new and in fact, he writes *"Tellingly, since 2007 Estonia has been operating a universal national digital identity scheme using blockchain. All government data about individuals is stored on a distributed ledger that individuals control and can pass to others."* He goes on to say that the personal digital signatures created are also used elsewhere in Europe. He indicates that mutual distributed ledgers which are enabled by blockchain are attractive for applications such as proof of identity. (Mainelli, 2017). Thus, Mainelli endorses the idea that blockchain technology may soon become synonymous with a secure means of identity and ownership. He, like other experts and proponents, is enthusiastic about the uses for this technology and proposes that it has a great many uses. Basing their development on blockchain would seem to be a positive step for the Virternity project as it is a technology which has already well-founded support.

In summary, the use of blockchain to enable the registration of ownership such as copyright and identity is spreading. Virternity's challenge could be perhaps to become a front runner in the inevitable race that will ensue as the use of this technology ramps up further. The opportunities are certainly there as is the potential for competition from other developers and the Virternity project can surely realise its aims in this area should it continue to pursue them.

Bibliography

Asharaf, S., & Adarsh, S. (2017). *Decentralized computing using blockchain technologies and smart contracts* (1st ed.). Hershey, PA : Information Science Reference.

Blockchain Based Anti-Counterfeit Solution. (2017). *Blockverify.io*. Retrieved 11 April 2017, from http://www.blockverify.io/

Blockchain solutions for Automotive. (2017). *Reply.com*. Retrieved 11 April 2017, from http://www.reply.com/en/content/thats-mine

Mainelli, M. (2017). Blockchain Will Help Us Prove Our Identities in a Digital World. *Harvard Business Review*.

Morabito, V. (2017). *Business innovation through blockchain* (1st ed.). Springer International Publishing.

Proof of Existence. (2017). *Proofofexistence.com*. Retrieved 11 April 2017, from https://proofofexistence.com/about

CHAPTER SIXTEEN

Virternity: Introduction of the field "temporary data" to the Virternity blockchain and combining existing blockchain databases into an integrated 3D blockchain

David Evans Bailey

This chapter discusses further the proposal of the Virternity project regarding making a temporary blockchain space where information can be deleted automatically after a set period which would be user selectable with the option to turn it into permanent data prior to this. The Virternity project asserts that one of the main blockchain advantages is the immutable and permanent nature of the data but that it is also a disadvantage in that it can include data that it is unnecessary for the user to keep forever. Additionally, the Virternity project proposes that the existence of multiple disparate blockchain databases prevents their functional interaction and free information flow in the global digital environment. They assert that they are open to all who want to join the project and combine their efforts, in particular, the idea of combining the existing blockchain databases into a single super-base or a large prototype of the new digital universe.

It is a fact that the goal of any blockchain is immutability and this is one of the foundations of its security. Bank professional Daniel Drescher describes this in his book *Blockchain Basics* where he says *"in order to protect the history of transactions from being manipulated by dishonest nodes, we want to prevent anyone from manipulating the history in the first place. If no one can change the history of transaction data, regardless of whether it is honest or dishonest, we do not have to fear that it can be manipulated at all. Hence, making the history of transaction data* unchangeable in the first place solves the problem." He continues pointing out that immutable data is effectively read-only and therefore cannot be changed. The inference is also that it cannot be deleted either and this is one of the cornerstones of the blockchain concept. The blockchain in his words enforces immutability by making even the smallest changes stand out, enforcing the idea that embedding a change requires rewriting a large part of it and it will be computationally expensive to do. (Drescher, 2017, pp.136-137). Drescher illustrates by these points and the way in which the hash structure of blockchain works that whilst it is not impossible to do, it will be obvious where blockchains have been tampered with. The entire idea of blockchain is that it does not require sophisticated software to protect it and that it is effectively self-protecting by its own structure and the way that it works. This allows distribution across nodes which may not all contain the same levels of security as each other or indeed as perhaps a banking system might but that the data is nevertheless as secure. Investment banker Imran Bashir confirms the immutability of blockchain in his book *Mastering Blockchain* where he says *"This is another key feature of blockchain: records once added onto the blockchain are immutable. There is the possibility of rolling back the changes but this is considered almost impossible to do as it will require an unaffordable amount of computing resources."* (Bashir, 2017, p. 23). This and other treatises on blockchain echo the same fundamental tenet of its creation which is that the data cannot be changed and that transactions, therefore, are never deleted or removed from the chain. The introduction of a temporary style of data which can be changed is something which is definitely a new concept and which appears to go against the accepted principles of all blockchain systems.

The fundamental question that the Virternity developers must ask themselves is whether blockchain is a panacea for all applications. There is certainly an element of recognising that no computer software is necessarily a one size fits all solution. Entrepreneur Gideon Greenspan and founder of *Coin Sciences*, a provider of private blockchain, writes about the idea of choosing whether to use blockchain as the technology of choice. In a blog on the subject, he contends that blockchains are 'overhyped'. He sets out five criteria on which to bases decisions as to the use of blockchain: Is a shared databased required? Are multiple writers modifying this database? Is there an absence of trust as in users must not be able to modify the transactions of others? Is there no trusted intermediary that can be used? Is interaction between transactions of mistrusting writers required? If all of these conditions can be fulfilled, then Greenspan contends that blockchain is the right answer. If they cannot then he argues that perhaps another solution is more appropriate. (Greenspan, 2015). This is sensible advice from a practitioner in the blockchain field. Virternity needs to ask these pertinent questions in the case of their temporary data proposal. On the surface, it would appear that temporary data would exist more in the form of notes and reminders which an individual might make for themselves thus negating the need for interaction with others with regard to that data. Greenspan concludes *"As I mentioned in the introduction, if your project does not fulfill **every single one of these conditions**, you should not be using a blockchain. In the absence of any of the first five, you should consider one of: (a) regular file storage, (b) a centralized database, (c) master–slave database* *replication, or (d) multiple databases to which users can subscribe."* (Greenspan, 2015). With respect to such applications as calendars, note systems and so forth, there are currently ample providers of these such as Microsoft Office incorporating Outlook and OneNote as an example. The take up of these products is extremely high, according to Microsoft's own figures, there are currently 400 million active users of Outlook ("Microsoft by the Numbers", 2017). Virternity developers perhaps need to ask the hard questions such as whether it is important to redevelop everything or is it better to tempt established market leaders into the fold? The merits of these approaches should be considered on a case by case basis and that would be a recommended way forward where there is already an existing buy in to well-established market products.

Microsoft Office's antecedents go back as far as 1990 meaning it has been over 27 years in development. ("History & Evolution of Microsoft Office Software", 2016). One cannot afford to ignore this track record and that of companies of a similar length of heritage. It should also be considered that the reach across hardware and software platforms of companies such as

Microsoft is extensive and their products are available on Apple as well as PC platforms. There is brand loyalty to consider among other things. Virternity's aims to become everything to everyone may not be borne out by the market history of IT software.

It is appropriate in this context to discuss the second point of attracting other blockchain databases to combine into one 3D database. There is a precedent for larger organisations of software to absorb other products into their fold. Google, for example, owns over 50 branded software products many of which were acquired by Google Inc. since its inception. (Alba, 2015). Microsoft owns less but as opposed to Google they rely upon their own products and have opted to absorb some competing brands such as Skype (Cassell, 2015). Facebook also owns several companies who either produced competing products or involved areas they wanted to expand into such as immersive VR with their acquisition of Oculus (Lwan, n.d.). History seems to indicate that large corporations with reputation and finance tend to acquire software offerings or competing products because they have the wherewithal to do so.

To get an idea of the number of blockchains there are currently it can be discovered that according to one website there are over 100 cryptocurrencies in existence and each of these will have their own blockchain. ("Crypto-Currency Market Capitalizations", 2017). In reality, the figures are probably far higher and there is no information currently to indicate that any of these have ever merged or been taken over. The market may not be mature enough for this nor perhaps large enough to support such takeovers and there may also be technical difficulties in merging blockchains of completely different origin and antecedent. This does not include any other kind of blockchain that might currently exist and records of these numbers are difficult to find. There is no definitive answer for Virternity in its ambition for a super-blockchain and the matter of whether what amounts to a virtual monopoly of technology is desirable would be another important question to be asked. Perhaps these are goals which can be realised once Virternity is firmly established in the marketplace and as a market leader which one might conjecture is a necessity in order to dictate the direction of the market. The examples of Microsoft,

Google and Facebook serve to illustrate that a certain level of market dominance is required as well as high capitalisation in order to persuade or indeed incentivize other enterprises to become part of your endeavour. There also remain legal obstacles such as Monopoly laws in countries such as the US. Overall this larger challenge for Virternity would seem to be very much dependent upon its successful implementation and growth. As an example, Google commenced operation in 1996 and received $25 million venture capital in 1999, in 2004 it became a public traded company and made its first purchase of YouTube in 2006 around 10 years after it was created. ("Google Timeline", 2017). The net worth of Google in March 2016 was around $498 billion. (Monica, 2016). This is an impressive growth curve in 20 years but one must note that it has taken Google time to achieve that figure and the size that it currently is. All of which leaves two notable points for Virternity, the first is that what they want to do in terms of conglomerate blockchain probably can be achieved once they are in a position of strength and the second is that this will probably take some time to realise. The key factors for Virternity are likely to be persistence and perseverance upon their given course considering that at the very least the technological factors for their virtual world and cryptocurrency weigh in their favour.

Bibliography

Alba, A. (2015). *The A to Z list of brands, companies Google's Alphabet owns. NY Daily News.* from http://www.nydailynews.com/news/world/z-list-brands-companies-google- alphabet-owns-article-1.2321981

Bashir, I. (2017). *Mastering Blockchain (1)* (1st ed.). Packt Publishing.

Cassell, W. (2015). *An Overview of Businesses Owned by Microsoft (MSFT). Investopedia.* from http://www.investopedia.com/articles/investin g/120715/overview-businesses-owned-microsoft.asp

Crypto-Currency Market Capitalizations. (2017). *Coinmarketcap.com.* Retrieved 29 January 2017, from https://coinmarketcap.com/

Drescher, D. (2017). *Blockchain basics* (1st ed.). Apress.

Greenspan, G. (2015). *Avoiding the pointless blockchain project | MultiChain. Multichain.com.* from http://www.multichain.com/blog/2015/11/avo iding-pointless- blockchain-project/

Google Timeline. (2017). *Datesandevents.org.* from http://www.datesandevents.org/events-timelines/18-google-timeline.htm

History & Evolution Of Microsoft Office Software. (2016). *The Windows Club.* from http://www.thewindowsclub.com/history-evolution-microsoft-office-software

Lwan, K. *9 Companies acquired and owned by Facebook | FBtutorial.com. FBtutorial.com.* from http://fbtutorial.com/9-companies-acquired-and-owned-by-facebook/

Microsoft by the Numbers. (2017). *Microsoft by the Numbers.* from https://news.microsoft.com/bythenumbers/

Monica, P. (2016). *Google is worth more than Apple again. CNNMoney.* from http://money.cnn.com/2016/05/12/investing/apple-google-alphabet-most-valuable/

CHAPTER SEVENTEEN

Virternity: Start-over of the Virternity space worldwide network. Virternity will become everyday practice of work and leisure in the developed countries

David Evans Bailey

This chapter discusses further the proposal of the Virternity project regarding their ideas that successful experiments with the advanced technologies of the future will make it possible to transfer and store all data from different information sources into the sole worldwide blockchain. They assert that the most important parts of material reality will be digitised and repeated in the virtuality and that the compound (mixed) reality devices will provide a permanent, wide exchange of information between the two realities in real time. They believe that it will take years before the majority of mankind will get used to life in such general compound reality as Virternity space, learning how to use its advantages and adapting economic, social and legal instruments. They infer that there will be a shift towards a parallel implementation in the virtual space; apartments and houses, cars, furniture, restaurants, medical consultations, fashion will perhaps exist primarily in the virtual reality. They propose that fewer resources will be needed to sustain economic growth and mass consumption. The luxury and superfluity will be transferred into the digital reality and that also education and entertainment may be transferred completely into the new reality. The essential part of personal life will follow the same direction. They hypothesise that Earth will gradually be digitised (and expanded) so that prominent sights of interest will be available from the comfort of the virtuality. They propose that animals (including pets) will be available in the virtual reality. The net result they assert is that there will be less demand upon the Earth's resources since enjoyment will be transferred to a virtual life. As a result, they argue that such things as travel, large scale construction, use of aviation and other such everyday activities may also be minimised and that ultimately consumption of energy will decline. They claim that this could reduce energy needs by as much as 60% to 80% of current usage.

These are very wide-ranging proposals and claims which at this time are obviously not proven. However, the probability of these assertions can be examined within the context of current developments and future potential. The degree to which any of these ideas can come to fruition is proportional to the take-up and use of VR, and developments in VR technology that enter the public domain. At the time of writing investment in VR is increasing and immersive technology is become more widely used. Applications for the use of VR are constantly being developed and research into the effects of VR itself has been ongoing since the 1990's. A recent article in *Fortune Magazine* plays down the VR sales figures from 2016 noting *"Sales figures for 2016 are in, and they're not exciting: The VR industry shipped 6.3 million devices and pulled in $1.8 billion in revenue, according to research firm Super*

Data. That's below expectations, though analysts say it isn't terrible for an emerging technology." (Roberts, 2017). However, that number of devices out in the mainstream is quite significant and although investors are doubtless disappointed since predictions were higher the indications are that the upwards trend will continue though perhaps not at the rate originally expected. An article in *Forbes* is more optimistic *"CCS Insights forecasts that the smartphone VR market will be worth $500 million this year, rising to approximately $1.4 billion by 2021. The analyst expects that 14 million smartphone VR headsets will be sold in 2017, increasing to 25 million in 2018 and up to a staggering 70 million by 2021. That's not to say that there's no legs in the dedicated VR headset area. CCS Insight estimates 1.2 million units were sold in 2016 and foresees sales growing to 22 million by 2021; in a dedicated VR market worth $7.7 billion."* (Lamkin, 2017). The prediction of 14 million smartphone VR headset sales for 2017 is a decisive jump and if it comes to fruition then it is likely to impact the number of applications using VR and the use of VR in general in an upwards direction. It would appear that analysts are looking for a four or five-year time span to bring VR into widespread use. The basis for almost all Virternity's expectations is predicated upon the continued take-up of VR. This foundation appears to be being put in place albeit not as quickly as was previously expected. Additionally, the *Hololens* and *Magic Leap* have not yet been released and the introduction of mixed reality technology will also affect the VR paradigm in ways that cannot currently be predicted with any accuracy.

Will there be a shift towards the use of Virtual space over physical space as the Virternity developers propose? A recent article in *Motherboard* made a case study of *Second Life*, which is the nearest VR platform to the Virternity model which has any kind of pedigree. *Second Life* began in 2003 which is over 14 years ago and according to editor Maiberg although the graphical quality is dated there is no other VR offering which is quite the same. He writes that it is a unique combination of the following *"It's a vast digital space many people can log into with their virtual avatars, only instead of going on wild adventures, slaying dragons and collecting epic swords, it just seems like a bunch of people hanging out in bars, offices,* galleries—*normal places.*" and that this normality and simulation of physical life is part of its appeal. He says that *Second Life* allows users to not only create their own avatars but also to shape and create the world they're in, importing their own 3D assets and modifying the world with a proprietary scripting language. This means that users make anything from 'sex dungeons' to political campaign headquarters. He notes that universities such as MIT and Stanford started building spaces in *Second Life* with the idea that virtual lectures and classes might be held in the digital space. *Second Life* users can also build and sell these creations to others. In fact, the article cites Ebbe Altberg, CEO of *Second Life*, as saying *"Last year, users redeemed $60 million (USD) from their Second Life businesses, and the virtual world's GDP is about $500 million, which is the size of some small countries."* (Maiberg, 2016). To quote a colloquial phrase that 'money talks' and given the sizeable investment in this virtual space and the degree of commerce being undertaken it proves to a large degree that a semi-VR existence is attractive to a fairly large number of people. That number of people being confirmed by Altberg as around 600,000 active users per month. Altberg told Maiberg that in spite of the legal regulatory and compliance work *Second Life* requires to administrate it and support the economy created without fraud and money laundering, they are more successful than any other virtual worlds who have tried and failed to emulate their success. Maiberg also notes *"it's a fascinating microcosm for both Internet and real world culture. And as a user-generated content platform, it still regularly produces really engaging, cool content, like a real life artist with a government grant to produce Second Life art, or a couple dudes playing live metal guitar for a Second Life audience from different parts of Japan."* (Maiberg, 2016). Maiberg also asserts that new competitors in the marketplace may find it difficult to persuade current users and business away from *Second Life* due to the level of financial investment and commitment they have already made. Even with the advent of immersive worlds some of those users may choose to remain loyal to their brand. *Second Life* is also moving in the immersive VR arena with a new world known as *Project Sansar* and planning to build on the success of its first enterprise and reach a broader audience. There are parallels to be drawn with

Virternity's ambitions and perhaps lessons to be learned. *Second Life* is a successful VR community and business enterprise which has realised some of the goals that Virternity aspires to. It certainly shows that there is a model of successful and thriving commerce within a virtual environment. Virternity could benefit and learn from a more in-depth study of this enterprise and that endeavour is to be recommended. *Second Life* users are perhaps selective in what they choose to spend time on in this virtual world and apparently, for many, this may be simply sexual adventure, but for others it can become a much more consuming addendum to their physical life or even subsume it. If nothing else, it certainly sets a pattern of future potential VR living. Virternity is certainly not the first developer with a desire to make inroads into the world of immersive and mixed reality. *AltspaceVR* is a community that has been setup with exactly that intention in mind. *AltspaceVR* bills itself as *"the leading social platform for virtual reality. Meet people from around the world, attend free live events, and play interactive games with friends."* ("Be there, together.", n.d.). AltspaceVR raised $10 million in funding for its platform in 2015 which is a sizeable investment of capital. (Roettgers, 2015). This indicates that there is faith in the potential of these types of platform and augers well for Virternity should they seek investment or capitalisation for their venture. AltspaceVR currently appears to consist of a community of room spaces where events or games are held. It is a kind of social networking in immersive space and is definitely in the early stages of its evolution. Whether it can compete with *Second Life's* new immersive world remains to be seen. However, the appearance of these types of endeavours endorses what Virternity wishes to do rather than detracts from it.

Having proposed the idea of the digitisation of Earth, it is useful to note that this is currently being undertaken by Google with the advent of Google Earth VR. An extension of Google Earth, the VR versions offers 3D immersive visuals of parts of Earth that can be explored using the *HTC Vive* currently. The experience is akin to being a giant looking down at a reduced size landscape. ("Google Earth VR", 2017). As an article in *The Verge* notes *"where Street View offers strings of photospheres collected by 360-degree cameras, users of Earth VR can virtually fly freely around a topographical reconstruction of the globe, or take guided tours of places like Manhattan and Monument Valley."* One of the attractions, according to the article, appears to be the future potential for embedding personalised content. ("You can now fly around Google Earth in virtual reality", 2016). The fact that Google has taken forward this initiative is significant and with the considerable resource that the company has at its disposal should mean that digitised assets of Earth's main attractions will continue to grow. This is in line with the expectations of Virternity. Whether those assets may become public domain for use in other virtual applications or worlds is not currently known. However, links to Google Maps are commonplace on websites as are API's to facilitate searches both from Google and from their map products, so the likelihood is that other developers will ultimately be able to tap into the 3D virtual content also.

To conclude an exploration of the transfer of modes of living to virtual reality it is useful to quote from Anthropologist Tom Boellstorf who conducted an in-depth study of *Second Life* in his book *Coming of Age in Second Life* which explored human behaviour in this virtual world. There are interesting analogies to be drawn between the virtual world and human reactions in the normal physical world, as for example in this extract he observes *"One resident described how when entering Second Life 'I log in and walk around my house. I love being here.' Another noted how 'having a place that I can go to when I want is a security for me . . . a refuge even.' A third resident, recovering from a serious injury in the actual world, spoke of his Second Life home by saying 'I built this place to relax. It's my place, it's mine.'"* (Boellstorff, 2015, pp. 100-101). It is thought provoking in that way that he designates users of the virtual world as residents and the implication is that part of them or at least their psyche resides there. This small abstract illustrating how humans can indeed become part of something that is not physical and still feel as if it belongs to them, and that they take away very normal human emotional reactions from it. It serves as a microcosm of understanding as to how virtual living can become analogous to real living for some. In another extract, the author notes how ordinary virtual life actually is *"Throughout my research I was struck by the banality of Second Life. Exotica could certainly be found...Yet everyday*

Second Life was also mundane creativity, conversation, intimacy, shopping, entertainment, even tedium. As one resident put it, 'that's the dirty secret of virtual worlds; all people end up doing is replicating their real lives.'" (Boellstorff, 2015, p. 239). The ease at which people can transfer the ordinary to the virtual is somewhat extraordinary according to Boellstorff. He characterises virtual worlds as places and not as networks and likens Second Life to an archipelago of islands and continents through which people connect and form relationships. Overall his comprehensive ethnographic study in many ways serves as an endorsement of the objectives of Virternity in that some of these are borne out in the real-life examples examined in the book. Whether Virternity can encourage the import of assets from other digital worlds or existences to their blockchain has been discussed elsewhere. What is more pertinent to consider is whether the broader goals outlined can be realised and whether humanity could consider that virtual reality is more home to them than actual physical reality. Outside of the realms of fiction and based on a real-life virtual world it would seem that the signs are definitely there that this could come to pass in some wise. How exactly this will or might happen remains to be seen once Virternity itself enters the arena of virtual reality.

Bibliography

Be there, together.. AltspaceVR Inc. Retrieved 17 April 2017, from https://altvr.com/

Boellstorff, T. (2015). *Coming of age in Second Life* (1st ed.).

Google Earth VR. (2017). *Vr.google.com.* from https://vr.google.com/earth/

Lamkin, P. (2017). *PlayStation VR Sales Near 1 Million With Huge VR Boom Predicted. Forbes.com.*, from https://www.forbes.com/sites/paullamkin/2017/02/27/playstation-vr-sales-near-1-million-with-huge-vr-boom-predicted/#1d39cbd79e6c

Maiberg, E. (2016). *Why Is 'Second Life' Still a Thing?. Motherboard.* Retrieved 16 April 2017, from https://motherboard.vice.com/en_us/article/why-is-second-life-still-a-thing-gaming-virtual-reality

Roberts, J. (2017). *VR Sales Numbers Are Wet Blanket on Adoption Hopes. Fortune.com.* from http://fortune.com/2017/02/19/virtual-reality-vr-sales/?iid=sr-link1

Roettgers, J. (2015). *AltspaceVR Raises $10 Million to Make Virtual Reality Social. Variety.* from http://variety.com/2015/digital/news/altspace

vr-raises-10-million-to-make-virtual-reality-social-1201551949/

You can now fly around Google Earth in virtual reality. (2016). *The Verge.* from http://www.theverge.com/2016/11/16/136435 50/google-earth-vr-htc-vive-release

CHAPTER EIGHTEEN

Virternity: Virtual reality games in the Virternity blockchain space

David Evans Bailey

This chapter discusses further the proposal of the Virternity project regarding their ideas that their virtual reality space will certainly create a space for all kinds of games, where in their words people can become different characters and play against other people. These are envisaged to be set in many different eras and contain also such experiences as visiting the Titanic, walking on the moon, flying through space will be available. People will be able to transform into fantastic forms of life, expanding the range of available experiences. Participation in the gladiatorial contests, or reenactments such searching for evidence at the crime scenes along with Sherlock Holmes or Miss Marple are envisaged with the advantage of 'respawn' if you happen to meet an untimely end. They contend that the experiences will be so 'real' that the experiences would be the equivalent of having encountered them in the physical world but without the risk of harm that might entail.

The current field of immersive and VR gaming is hard to enumerate or find accurate figures for. One article for *UploadVR* in June 2016 listed 107 VR games for Steam although how many of these were fully immersive taking full advantage of the Vive's functionality is another matter. (Feltham, 2016). Equally when gaming reviews mention the 30 best games for the PS4 VR then it is fair to assume there are many more ("30 essential PlayStation VR games", 2017). What is certain is that the market for VR and immersive gaming empowered by the hardware currently available and in the hands of consumers is a burgeoning one. This assumption is supported by sales figures for the PS4 VR which between its launch in October 2016 and February 2017 sold almost 1 million units. (Wingfield, 2017). Since the PS4 VR is a gaming console and dedicated mainly to gaming then it is safe to expect that the VR games for it will be available in sufficient quantities and variety to attract consumers. In addition to this many of the games offer cooperative or multiplayer options which allow competition or collaboration between players around the world thus addressing in part another of Virternity's ambitions in this regard. (Imel, 2017). Overall the conclusion must be that immersive VR gaming is not 'new news' as such and that Virternity will be entering an existing market rather than attempting to make inroads into virgin territory.

The concept of Online gaming worlds is not new either. Many have been in existence for several years. These are called MMOG's or Massive Multiplayer Online Games (or often MMORPG – Massive Multiplayer Online Role Playing Games) of which well-known and notable examples are *World of Warcraft* and *Minecraft*. Sociologist William Bainbridge describes *World of Warcraft* in his book, *The Warcraft Civilisation*, as *"World of Warcraft (WoW), the most popular massively multiplayer online role-playing game (MMORPG), created by Blizzard Entertainment. By December 2008, WoW had eleven million players in North America, Europe, and Asia."*

(Bainbridge, 2010, p. 4). This sizeable online population dedicated to one particular world is impressive and indicates the popularity of these kinds of online multiplayer gaming worlds. Bainbridge states that *WoW* is far from just being an online role-playing game but is indeed an online world, a community in its own right. From that point of view, it illustrates that Virternity can emulate this type of successful endeavour should they wish to attempt it. Bainbridge goes on to elaborate what makes *WoW* a game as opposed to just an online community *"World of Warcraft has the essential quality that people generally associate with games: competition. Players must struggle against adversity to increase many point scores, of which the most crucial is experience, which takes them up a graded series of levels. Attaining a high level is a source of pride."* (Bainbridge, 2010, p. 6). This is an essential point worth noting to delineate the difference between online living and online gaming. In normal living, there are struggles but perhaps most people do not live their lives as if they are continually entering the field of competition and this can be seen in other VR worlds like *Second Life*. However, a gaming environment apparently, according to Bainbridge, must have the essential attributes of acquisition and attainment. This would be a point to note if Virternity is to venture into this gaming arena. *WoW* also fits the mould of fantasy players and fantastic creatures. MMOG's are being launched on a regular basis. An article in *PCGamesN* outlines 11 new games for 2017 that it recommends the majority of consist of fantasy types of worlds and one which is a tank world appropriately named *World of Tanks* ("New MMORPGs 2017: 11 new and upcoming MMOs worth looking out for", 2017). Given the extensive work that is likely to be required to service this type of game, this indicates that there is an ongoing market and appetite among the consumers of such offerings which is undiminished. Virternity could safely assume that were they to enter this market then they would have a readily available potential public.

The level of realism that these games supply is currently technology dependent. Most of the games and online world's supply graphical content which is in keeping with what was available when they were set up or what is now available in the marketplace. Though graphical content is a restriction, it doesn't appear to have diminished or even dictated the demand for gaming in general and online gaming in particular. The figures cited above for *WoW* which are comparatively high in terms of users illustrate that realism, as such, is not necessarily a particular factor in dictating whether or not people will subscribe to the service or play the game. Virternity contends that realism is part of the content package that they wish to supply. Two questions need to be posed, the first is whether the technology is capable of doing this at the point of entry into the gaming field and the second is whether it is actually necessary? The real issue is whether the aim with gaming is to suspend reality or to encompass it. Both are valid arguments but it must be recognised that this is a choice. Cartoonist Scott McCloud illustrates this point most clearly in his book *Understanding Comics* where he says *"Thus when you look at a photo or realistic drawing of a face-- you see it as the face of another. But when you enter the world of the cartoon- -you see yourself. I believe this the primary cause of our childhood fascination with cartoons. Though other factors such as universal identification, simplicity and the childlike features of many cartoon characters also play a part. The cartoon is a vacuum into which our identity and awareness is pulled. An empty shell that we inhabit which enables us to travel into another realm. We don't just observe the cartoon, we become it."* (McCloud, 1994, p. 36). In other words, to identify with a character in a cartoon often requires simplification of the features in order to impose your own identity upon it. The more realistic the character becomes the less a person imposes themselves on it and the more they see that character as someone else. This may illustrate in part the attraction of games and online worlds where the graphics are not entirely realistic. It is potentially this simplification that allows the person to discard their real-world identity and assume their online role. Virternity developers need to consider points such as these when making their choices. Whilst it may be an attractive proposition to produce a *Matrix* like (Wachowski & Wachowski, 1999) quality of realism where the digital is indistinguishable from the physical world reality, more consideration should go into whether this is either desirable or even necessary before such decisions are made.

One of the factors that should be explored further is Virternity's contention that participants are without risk from harm. Whilst the risk of physical harm in VR appears to be minimal apart from issues like motion sickness and other physical symptoms that might occur when using VR, there is the potential for psychological harm and this needs to be assessed when promoting any kind of online experience gaming or otherwise. A recent study into Internet Addiction (AI) of users of *Wow* found that *"Our study is one of the first to deal with addiction and engagement among (expert) high-level players of MMORPG. 93.7% played on level 85 (at the time the highest level at World of Warcraft); nevertheless, only 3.1% are addicted according to the "Internet Addiction Scale", suggesting that even 'hardcore' gaming does not automatically link to addiction."* (Bishop, 2015, p. 12). This is an encouraging statistic since IA is an obvious area of concern when linked to gaming. On the other hand, a study in 2006 regarding seizures induced by these kinds of games concluded that in the limited number of cases based on a small sample size studied MMORPG games had indeed been a contributing factor in epileptic types of seizures. (Chuang, 2006). Another study revealed a link between aggression and online gaming addictive behaviour. It noted *"In the results of this study, aggression was the strongest determinant on game addiction among the psychosocial variables. People who are aggressive express their aggression through diverse channels. Online games can be one of the means to reveal their aggression because online games contain some aggressive factors."* (Jeong, Kim, Lee, & Lee, 2016, p. 3775). Thus, game content coupled with a predisposition for aggressive behaviour could act as a fuel to drive antisocial behaviour in a particular individual, and this could also be allied to factors of loneliness and depression. The person could become addicted to games as a way of harnessing their aggression and overcoming their loneliness and depression. The psychological factors of engaging in virtual gaming seem to some degree related to the disposition and mental state of the individual. It can be concluded that harmful effects cannot, therefore, be entirely ruled out (either physical or mental) and due diligence needs to be observed when implementing such gaming environments; something Virternity developers will need to take note of.

With these additionally proposed ventures into the online world of gaming, can Virternity indeed become everything to everyone? Their overall aim seems to be to become an encompassing online world, perhaps a real-life incarnation of *OASIS* in *Ready Player One* (Cline, 2011). Given these extensive and what must be long term ambitions it is not possible to say whether they can or even will achieve all of them. The challenge that Virternity has set themselves is extensive. To focus simply on an online gaming world alone would require an investment of not an inconsiderable amount of time and money. Can a gaming world or even multiple worlds be achieved in Virternity? Most certainly the actuality of these types of worlds in the public domain is already a fact and Virternity will be entering what seems to be a ready market for these should they decide to add this to their portfolio of offerings. An open question is what also will attract others away from the online worlds they already frequent and thus have a 'brand loyalty'? This is certainly one that Virternity will have to answer.

Bibliography

30 essential PlayStation VR games. (2017). *Digital Spy.* from http://www.digitalspy.com/gaming/feature/a7 99244/best-playstation-vr-games/

Bainbridge, W. (2010). *The Warcraft civilization* (1st ed.). Cambridge, Ma.: MIT Press.

Bishop, J. (2015). *Psychological and social implications surrounding internet and gaming addiction* (1st ed.). Hershey, PA : Information Science Reference.

Chuang, Y. (2006). Massively Multiplayer Online Role-Playing Game-Induced Seizures: ANeglected Health Problem in Internet Addiction. *Cyberpsychology & Behavior, 9*(4), 451-456. http://dx.doi.org/10.1089/cpb.2006.9.451

Cline, E. (2011). *Ready Player One.* New York: Crown Publishers.

Feltham, J. (2016). *Steam has 107 VR games on sale — and here are the 6 best. VentureBeat.* Retrieved 17 April 2017, from https://venturebeat.com/2016/06/25/steam-has-107-vr-games-on-sale-and-here-are-the-6-best/

Imel, D. (2017). *The best multiplayer VR games. VR Source.* Retrieved 17 April 2017, from http://vrsource.com/best-multiplayer-vr-games-8810/

Jeong, E., Kim, D., Lee, D., & Lee, H. (2016). A Study of Digital Game Addiction from Aggression, Loneliness and Depression Perspectives. *2016 49Th Hawaii International Conference On System Sciences (HICSS).* http://dx.doi.org/10.1109/hicss.2016.470

McCloud, S. (1994). *Understanding comics*. New York: HarperPerennial.

New MMORPGs 2017: 11 new and upcoming MMOs worth looking out for. (2017). *PCGamesN*. from https://www.pcgamesn.com/new-mmos

Wachowski, L., & Wachowski, L. (1999). *The Matrix*. from http://www.imdb.com/title/tt0133093/

Wingfield, N. (2017). *Popularity of Sony's PlayStation VR Surprises Even the Company*. *Mobile.nytimes.com*. from https://mobile.nytimes.com/2017/02/26/business/sony-playstation-vr-sales.html?_r=0&referer=https://www.google.ca/

CHAPTER NINETEEN

Virternity: First successful transition of the persons into the Virternity space (as sui juris individuals with social responsibility, work, social contacts, etc.) Transitions of persons into the virtual part of the Virternity space becomes everyday practice. Immortality in Virternity available in practice for all.

David Evans Bailey

This paper discusses further the proposal of the Virternity project regarding the transition of persons into the Virternity world. Virternity asserts that for these people there will be no technological or psychological barrier for a complete transition from one world to another. They contend that when their physical body is failing they will continue life in a digital existence and that many older people will have already spent many years in this virtual world and the transition will not be difficult to adjust to. They speculate that a growing number of people will make a decision to permanently move to the virtual reality where they will benefit from the adaptation to not being prone to the effects of a physical existence any longer. They envisage a smooth transfer developing the virtual component of their personality in such a way that the transition will simply be a continuation of their existence. Thus, they hope to answer the question of human immortality and argue that the physical body is a stepping stone to assuming a virtual digital existence. Should this aim be successful Virternity argues that it will bring major changes to Mankind and how life on earth is organised, in terms of population, food, climate control. They suggest that the planet surface will be used for child rearing and family life and other pursuits allowing it to naturally recover. There will be a reduction in any kind of travel and transportation. Physical life needs will become limited. Robotics could have developed to perform such activities as surgery which are controlled from VR. They propose that the physical world will have less 'unpleasant' experiences and that a small cadre of people will choose to remain and support those living in VR and leading to a sustainable future for civilisation and the planet overall. In summary, Virternity hopes to provide the solution to 'death' and the quest for eternal life. An almost reverse vector may occur where physical avatars would be controlled by virtual humans to experience the physical sensations of the planet.

This far-reaching set of aims suggests new sets of paradigms for the human race and humanity. Such overarching goals were before this only the subject of science fiction and even in those fictional works envisage varying degrees of success. Whilst Virternity paints a utopian vision of the virtual future, fiction has had a tendency to see it otherwise with more dystopic outcomes imagined. In *The Matrix* (Wachowski & Wachowski, 1999) an iconic movie about virtual humanity, machines have resorted to using human bodies as power cells to drive a fully realistic simulation of Earth. The simulation is naturally broken by those who discover its true intent and work towards dismantling it. However, the virtual reality imbues those within it with powers that are not obtainable in the physical world, such as distorting time and running up walls. The war between humans and artificial intelligence continues through the series of *Matrix* movies but the ultimate goal becomes the dismantling of the virtual world rather than sustaining it and a return to physical living. The virtual becomes rejected seen as an imprisonment of the consciousness rather than the fulfilment of an ultimate freedom. The fictional novel *Ready Player One* (Cline, 2011) is a little more benign in outlook in that the virtual world OASIS is created by humans for the use of and for the good of humanity. There are many parallels between what is envisaged by Virternity and the fictional virtual realm of OASIS. Most human activity takes place within the OASIS virtual environment and physical living is relegated to a matter of survival of bodily necessities rather than the pursuits that humanity experiences today. Education and almost all interaction are done in the virtual world. However, the dystopic element is an organisation that is attempting to use OASIS to enslave and control people. An escalating battle between the forces of good and evil ensues and eventually, the virtual world is freed for all. However, the message from the book is not a clear endorsement of this style of existence although it elicits many attractions for it in the sense of powers and abilities that can be assumed in virtual reality that are not present in the physical world. The book leaves the reader with the sense that the virtual and physical worlds will somehow continue to exist in harmony now that the attempts to subvert it have been defeated. It perhaps and endorsement of virtual living but without the idea that humans will ultimately become free of their physical selves. Even as far back as the beginning of the 20th century E.M Forster wrote of a machine-controlled world in *The Machine Stops* (Forster, n.d.). Whilst it does not take place in a virtual realm, humans live underground in isolated chambers and all of their needs are serviced by a vast machine. Contact between people is reserved for the use of video style chats through television globe devices which are arguably therefore virtual. This solitary existence continues unabated for all until the machine malfunctions and it comes to an abrupt conclusion. Some of humanity rediscover the surface of the Earth as a viable place to live thus once again rejecting the virtual life. The unfortunate nature of these styles of fictional accounts is that it can predispose such encompassing virtual styles of existence to a certain amount of cynicism which Virternity would have to overcome. As can been seen the conclusion of these tales tends to be one that ultimately restores humans to a physical existence rather than move them into a virtual one. One might also view works like *Ready Player One* as a potential melting pot of ideas that seem laudable at the time but that can go very much awry when the wrong kind of individuals become involved. Obviously, because they are works of fiction there is an element of jeopardy and salvation that is required and thus it removes them to some extent from the banal realities of normal life.

In truth, the extensive ambitions of Virternity would take some time to realise, assuming that they actually can be brought to pass. The issue of transferring a human to cyberspace has been reviewed in other chapters of this series along with the philosophical issues surrounding it. Rather than revisit this ground it is sufficient to note that what is currently known is that this transfer has not yet been achieved. Methods of doing so have been hypothesised in some detail but the actuality of it is still some way off. Until a serious attempt has been made and perhaps succeeded these remain only ambitions. With an earth population of around 7 billion people and rising, there are many logistical points to be considered were the transfer even to become possible. The matter of computer storage is one obvious area which would need careful exploration. How much storage would one hypothetical virtual human require and then how much would that translate into for 7 billion people? Where would these data centres be located? Who would administrate them and how? What fault tolerance and resilience would of necessity have to be put in place in order to mitigate the risk of losing the entire digitised population of earth? And the corollary what security measures would be needed to prevent the deliberate annihilation of the digitised humanity?

What is to prevent the systematic deletion of individuals that a faction of the population dislikes, a kind of digital ethnic cleansing? These and much more are questions that very necessary in a serious proposal to replace the physical existence of humans with a virtual one. It is not just a matter of the technology required to digitise a human but the ability to sustain that, to manage it and to protect it that becomes important. It would be expected that this to be the subject of some debate and detailed planning before it can be put into practice. Whoever controls all of that virtual real estate could also potentially have the ability to manipulate the population of earth or as it would be, digitised earth, as never before. It is already a matter of recorded scientific study that VR and particularly immersive VR is prone to manipulation or at least to influence people beyond those techniques that are available in the physical world. Stanford University, a leading proponent of psychological research in VR has undertaken numerous research projects which clearly establish this. Manipulating height, colour, eye gaze, body mimicry and many other factors in virtual reality can influence people in negative and positive ways. Changing a politician's virtual features to resemble the person's own by 40% result in more empathy and being more likely to be swayed by that politician's opinions, just as an example of something that is easily achievable in VR. (Blascovich, & Bailenson, 2011). As fictional works show, Utopia always has another side to it, and this is also borne out by the history of planet Earth and the ravages of two World Wars the second of which was started on account of the attempt to subvert humanity to a dystopian rule of a fascist regime. The potential for events to go down the wrong path cannot be understated and indeed should be clearly stated in order for such pitfalls to be avoided and the potential issues to be addressed.

The interesting notion of digital humans controlling actual avatars is addressed in the film *Avatar* (Cameron, 2009) where humans enter the bodies of alien beings on another planet and become those bodies in order to communicate and interact with the local alien population. The idea is at least hypothesised in fiction although the actual mechanism of achieving this is not elucidated. There is a certain irony in having achieved digitisation of a human being to then attempt to control a physical identity from the digital self.

Projects to develop robots under mind control have been proposed. In 2014, researchers Butt and Stanacevic put forward a design in a conference paper which would use brainwaves to send control signals to a robot that could be used for such applications as the aid of paralysed patients. (Butt, & Stanacevic, 2014). In 2015 another research project tested a neuro-headset using which subjects were able to relay a limited set of commands to a robot to move in different directions. (Malki, Yang, Wang, & Li, 2015). Naturally, a digitised human or intelligence would not require such a device and would be able to transmit commands directly through a digital network, making the idea of this in theory perfectly possible.

The implications for humanity, in general, are great if some of Virternity's ultimate aims come to pass. Virternity perhaps needs to recognise that a great deal of unknown factors lie ahead not the least of which are the implications of what they want to do technically. It is evident that the potential positive outcomes of a digitised human race have been considered but at the same time, the potential negative outcomes need to be known and guarded against. With such a substantial change in the entire fabric of society, there is much more groundwork to be done. The likelihood is that incremental change will occur as VR technology becomes increasingly mainstream and Virternity comes online. At that point, future developments in technology will to some degree dictate the direction of the project. It has been noted before that this presents many challenges to overcome. Virternity needs to attain some pedigree within the field and establish itself as not only a leader in VR terms but then demonstrate that it can overcome the challenges with which it has presented itself and without endangering the ultimate future of humanity in the process.

Bibliography

Blascovich, J., & Bailenson, J. (2011). *Infinite reality.* New York: William Morrow.

Butt, A., & Stanacevic, M. (2014). Implementation of Mind Control Robot. *IEEE Long Island Systems, Applications And Technology (LISAT) Conference 2014.* http://dx.doi.org/10.1109/lisat.2014.6845218

Cameron, J. (2009). *Avatar. IMDb.* Retrieved 18 April 2017, from http://www.imdb.com/title/tt0499549/

Cline, E. (2011). *Ready Player One.* New York: Crown Publishers.

Forster, E. M. (n.d.). *The Machine Stops.* First published in the Oxford and Cambridge Review, November 1909.

Malki, A., Yang, C., Wang, N., & Li, Z. (2015). Mind guided motion control of robot manipulator using EEG signals. *2015 5Th International Conference On Information Science And Technology (ICIST).* http://dx.doi.org/10.1109/icist.2015.7289033

Wachowski, L., & Wachowski, L. (1999). *The Matrix.* Retrieved from http://www.imdb.com/title/tt0133093/

CHAPTER TWENTY

Virternity: Humanity existing simultaneously in the both physical and virtual reality

David Evans Bailey

This chapter discusses further the proposal of the Virternity project regarding the idea of real and virtual people (people solely in virtual reality) communicating in the Virternity space. They assert that such things as family memories can be mutually shared through the proposed ability to see each other's memories. With a plethora of virtual experts, they envisage that this can be passed on through generations and that artists of all disciplines can continue to be productive in virtual space. Equally, scientists can continue their virtual research. Time will no longer be of the essence as people have the necessary time to complete projects and studies and fulfil their potential. Virtual people could also control mechanisms in conditions that could be dangerous for ordinary people. They also propose sending virtual people on missions to explore space and also allow for faster space travel. Time travel will be effected by the ability to return to past events and memories with the ability to view them internally or externally to the event. Actual decision modelling could be made to alter the course of events or even to revisit and relive past events with a different outcome. They see there is the possibility for a multitude of games and that perhaps will be made as virtual games without the catastrophic outcomes. Their expectation is that this existence will lead to new philosophical questions and paths of thinking. Although they envisage a positive and green field world of opportunity unfettered by the restrictions of physical earth, they assert that they don't expect a paradise on virtual Earth. They anticipate new economic, political and social challenges of the new society, unimaginable now along with new weapons, new forms of torture, new mental illnesses and offences. To counter these, they expect there to be people and programs engaged in law enforcement, investigation and punishment; in the same way that viruses created the anti-virus industry. They even anticipate that there may be a new form of unspecified death but that the main angst of the present-day life: physical death (as well as old age, infirmity and illnesses) and depletion of resources (poverty, wars and fierce competition as well) will become irrelevant.

These concluding and wide-ranging claims are in part realistic and in part pure speculation. There is an element of pragmatism at least in the statements made. The most important of these is the envisaged idea of humans remaining in their physical selves but coexisting in virtual reality. This might be expected to be the first milestone of any such endeavour. The dual existence of humans in virtuality is already *de facto* with worlds such as *Second Life*, where this coexistence is already happening. Anthropologist Tom Boelstorff describes it thus *"The relationship between the virtual and the human is not a 'post' relationship where one term displaces another; it is a relationship of coconstitution. Far from it being the case that virtual worlds herald the emergence of the posthuman, in this book I argue that it is in being virtual that we are human. Virtual worlds reconfigure selfhood and sociality, but this is only possible because they rework the virtuality that characterizes human being in the actual world."* (Boellstorff, 2015, p. 29). His argument is that people reconfigure themselves in virtual space due to the additional latitude they get to assume a different persona, identity with many other attributes. This brings up the interesting question that the coexistence that Virternity proposes may in effect be one person with two different identities, the same personality but taking advantage of the different constraints that the virtual existence presents. If a human was to ever be able to completely transfer to virtual space would they be the same person even then? There are many assumptions for which the complete answer is unknown since it has so far never happened. It can, however, be conjectured upon what we do know through the research and observation of others who have studied virtual worlds.

Researcher Joseph S. Clark writing in chapter 7 of *Creating Second Lives* notes some fundamental points about virtual worlds which have relevance "As we create and inhabit spaces within three-dimensional virtual worlds, we simultaneously create unique places that foster the development of communities, as users return to and inhabit the same electronic locales over time. These sites then become aspects of identity for both avatars and the human beings behind them, in much the same way that one identifies with a neighborhood, workplace, or hometown in the non-virtual world." In effect participation in virtual communities to a degree mirror the physical world and the communities that are familiar in those spaces. He implies that the creation of these worlds always includes natural elements such as real life nature (grass, trees, landscape) and that this emphasizes the importance to virtual participation of these things. It is almost as if there is a transference of 'reality' to the virtual space and although there may be the unfamiliar people also want the things that are familiar. He also goes on to assert "And as with other media— from advertisements and architecture to chat rooms and wikis— these virtual places become important means of cultural transmission, political activity, and creative work." (Ensslin, & Muse, 2011, p. 145). Thus, indicating clearly that there is the evident building of a virtual culture within a virtual world. Humans will therefore inevitably impose their sense of community and cultural and social activity within a digital realm. However, if Virternity's objectives were realised, at least in part, then there may be a cadre of people who have more familiarity with the virtual world than the physical world in which their bodies reside. In this case, might it not be true that new cultural forms and norms may emerge? At this point it cannot be predicted or even envisaged what may emerge from prolonged exposure to a virtual environment that contains its own paradigms and if that becomes normality for an individual. As Clark says virtual worlds have already engendered different types of behaviour "A space such as Second Life generates new forms of social behavior, or twists on old ones: 'griefing' (pranks and harassment), cultural collisions between humanoid avatars and 'furries' (animal-like avatars), and gender-bending are just some of the more well known." (Ensslin, & Muse, 2011, p. 147). These minor examples nevertheless point perhaps to some deeper changes in the psyche of those who become involved in virtual existences for a prolonged extent of time. This is particularly true of full immersion where the factor of 'presence' puts the person firmly in the virtual space and it becomes all the more real to them. Under these conditions, it is entirely conceivable that there may be changes in social attitudes and behaviour which are consistent with the new virtual environment and abilities with which it endows the person. Clark supports this idea when he writes "The experience of virtual reality may not even be clearly distinct for the user. Whereas there is a tendency toward disassociation and disembodiment that arises from a camera-like, third person view, Stewart and Nicholls argue that the virtual body and an engaging virtual narrative can result in 'one phenomenal body' that melds the virtual and the real identities." (Ensslin, & Muse, 2011, p. 148). This point about virtual embodiment has also been made by media theorists such as Melanie Chan who in her article *Virtual Reality* asserts that virtual environments are experienced through the body and not simply just perceived. (Chan, 2014, pp. 134-5). She means that even though the individual may not be able to see their own body in virtual space they nevertheless feel as if they are in that space and become part of it. Thus, the identity of the person is merged with that of the digital persona and becomes, to all intents and purposes, one identity.

Another prominent theorist Mark Hansen discusses the idea that virtual space is felt within the body itself rather than simply through visual senses alone. This embodiment produces an affective response within the physical body itself to what is being experienced and gives the sensation of being actually within the virtual space. (Hansen, 2006, p. 232). The argument is that if a person feels as if they are in the virtual space they will become part of that space, merged with it in some way for the duration of the exposure to it. This supports some of what Virternity anticipates will happen to prolonged exposure to their world and experience of virtual environments by others tends to support that view.

On the matter of crime and cyberspace, Professor of Criminology Sara M Smyth notes in a journal article that one of the first cyberspace crimes was, in fact, a cyberspace rape by a character named "Mr Bungle" who utilised a virtual voodoo doll to perform offensive acts upon other users of the virtual world *LamdaMOO*. She writes that effective action against the offender was difficult if not impossible to take since he continued to return under various pseudonyms even though banished from the world. Thus, her assertion is that *"Nonetheless, the moral of the MOO story is that, as Lessig puts it, 'cyberspace will not take care of itself,' and that some form of regulation is needed to prevent the technology-generated environments from being exploited by antisocial characters and criminals."* (Smyth, 2009, pp. 32-33). She implies that there has to be some regulation with consequences that are effective either within the virtual world or upon the offender in their physical persona. This kind of action is clearly evident in Acts of Parliament passed to prevent cyberbullying and harassment in countries such as the UK and New Zealand, where reverting to normal real-world jurisprudence is necessary to prevent and deal with offenders. However, she also then goes on to cite Lessig as pointing out that 'code is law' in that the use of passwords and other code that can be changed and effectively lock offenders out of cyberspace can also be effective. (Smyth, 2009, p. 36). What her article shows is that this is an ongoing debate. Some worlds such as *Second Life* have established rules which, for example, prohibit the killing of another Second Lifer. It is obvious from these examples that rules are necessary and follow from any endeavour that involves humans in a community. Whether these can be entirely enforceable only in VR is another matter which is still in debate. In their article, *Ethical Issues in Second Life* Botterbusch and Talab write of a number of notable examples of virtual world crime which include: a woman killing her husband's avatar in a computer game because he had 'dumped' her in real life, a woman plotting the real-life abduction of her *Second Life* boyfriend and a boy who had swindled $360,000 of virtual currency. (Botterbusch, & Talab, 2009, p. 7). The justice and police actions were nevertheless carried out in the physical world rather than the digital. It is safe to assume that the more people become engaged in virtual living the more it will align to problems found in the real world and at the same time engender unique problems of the virtual world which are part of the proprietary properties that ensue from virtual life. The same statement can be applied to crime, there will inevitably be crime in cyberspace and in the Virternity space and the developers recognise this fact. They will have the opportunity to both invoke real-world legal proceedings in the country where the perpetrator resides as well as virtual justice actions. How these virtual justice actions will work and what they will be is part of the challenge of administrating and creating such a virtual community. It is obvious that virtual living cannot be without consequences for those who cross the boundaries, but what those boundaries are and how they are dealt with is currently a matter for conjecture.

One last consideration is that of new forms of death in Virternity or what one might term as virtual death. Attorney Jordan L Walbesser writes in an article *Finding Meaning in the Death of Virtual Identities* that *"In order for virtual identities to be as useful as physical-world identities (as well as compatible with our traditional legal notions), credentials need to be separated from identity and made transferable from one entity to another."* (Walbesser, 2014, p. 72). The reason for this is that the credentials of the person exist beyond the loss of the identity. This is important for others to manage their affairs which would include their digital affairs and who owns or has access to these digital assets is important. For those with assets in cyberspace, there may have real or intrinsic value and control of these following and individual's death is an issue which must be addressed. Walbesser argues that technical solutions do not solve these problems and that legal frameworks are required to address these. He asserts that credentials will need to be transferable from one entity to another although what these credentials should be is also a matter to be resolved. Further to the issue of death in cyberspace as regards the identity held in digital form this may be simply a matter of deletion to remove that person from the system or world. If, however, as is mooted by Virternity that entity is an actual person then the deletion amounts to a similar act as the death of a physical human and one must assume cannot, therefore, be viewed lightly. The issue of personality within the context and framework of digital cyberspace and the rights of that digital person is likely to be no small topic of debate.

What can be summarised is that there are many serious issues to be resolved around life and death in the virtual world. Virternity enters this with enthusiasm that is clear but this is also tempered by pragmatism. However ultimately each step that is taken towards a more stable virtual existence will require extensive study, formulation and codification. The matters that have been raised in this final chapter are not small things but potentially unleash a vast array of further questions that need to be answered. These can only be answered over the fullness of time and the continued development of Virternity's virtual world.

Bibliography

Boellstorff, T. (2015). *Coming of age in Second Life* (1st ed.).

Botterbusch, H., & Talab, R. (2009). Ethical Issues in Second Life. *Techtrends*, *53*(1), 9-13. http://dx.doi.org/10.1007/s11528-009-0227-4

Chan, M. (2014). *Virtual Reality: Representations in Contemporary Media* (1st ed.). New York: Bloomsbury Academic USA.

Ensslin, A., & Muse, E. (2011). *Creating second lives* (1st ed.). New York: Routledge.

Hansen, M. (2006). *New philosophy for new media* (1st ed.). Cambridge, Mass.: MIT.

Smyth, S. (2009). Back to the Future: Crime and Punishment in Second Life. *Rutgers Computer And Technology Law Journal*, *36*(1), 18-72.

Walbesser, J. (2014). FINDING MEANING IN THE DEATH OF VIRTUAL IDENTITIES. *Buffalo Intellectual Property Law Journal*, *10http://www.citethisforme.com/cite/journal*, 70-91.

EPILOGUE

David Evans Bailey

What can be concluded for the future of Virternity? At the time of writing and closure of this book, there is, as the often-repeated sports adage implies, everything to play for. Virternity enters a world of opportunities at this time in the history of virtual reality. This medium, maligned in the past due to its supreme failure to launch, appears to be finally reaching escape velocity. The moment when it might finally break free of the gravitational pull of the technological strings that hampered it before and launches itself into a perpetual orbit of innovation seems nigh. Much is made of the day when VR will go mainstream, and indeed in 2016 that particular goal appears to have become well within the grasp of the investors and developers who have been striving to achieve it. It is, however, true that a critical mass of a sort is required in order to arrive at a point where it becomes part of everyday life, much as the smartphone or social media have done in the past. Given the amount of investment, the impetus to succeed and the actuality of hardware platforms that can actually deliver it, then this time it seems safe to predict that VR is here to stay. Many of the stated goals of Virternity are achievable or will be within a relatively short space of time. Given the searching nature of man and the drive to do the impossible, that impossible soon becomes probable and eventually becomes part of the fabric of our existence. There is no doubt that given enough of the right investment and the technically competent people to carry it out, Virternity can succeed. For the moment, however, nothing else is known. Virternity awaits, in the background, preparing to launch. To say much more than that would simply be pure speculation on my part. However, having reviewed the aims and goals of Virternity in the context of what is known in terms of research, expert opinion, case studies and more, it is safe to say that Virternity can succeed. Whether they will succeed is a matter for history and not for this book. Whatever happens, once Virternity does emerge from its chrysalis and starts to fly it seems destined to make an impact on the future of VR to come.

FULL LIST OF REFERENCES

2016 VR Porn Statistics Say VR Is Hot. (2017). *VRCircle.* Retrieved 13 March 2017, from https://www.vrcircle.com/2016-vr-porn-statistics-say-vr-is-hot/

30 essential PlayStation VR games. (2017). *Digital Spy.* from http://www.digitalspy.com/gaming/feature/a799244/best-playstation-vr-games/

8i. (2017). *8i.* Retrieved 12 March 2017, from https://8i.com/

Ahn, S. (2016). Becoming a network beyond boundaries: Brain-Machine Interfaces (BMIs) as the actor-networks after the internet of things. *Technology In Society*, *47*, 49-59. http://dx.doi.org/10.1016/j.techsoc.2016.08.003

Ahn, S., Bailenson, J., & Park, D. (2014). Short- and long-term effects of embodied experiences in immersive virtual environments on environmental locus of control and behavior. *Computers In Human Behavior*, *39*, 235-245. http://dx.doi.org/10.1016/j.chb.2014.07.025

Alba, A. (2015). *The A to Z list of brands, companies Google's Alphabet owns. NY Daily News.* from http://www.nydailynews.com/news/world/z-list-brands-companies-google- alphabet-owns-article-1.2321981

Anderson, G. (2016). New digital money. *Acuity*.

Asharaf, S., & Adarsh, S. (2017). *Decentralized computing using blockchain technologies and smart contracts* (1st ed.). Hershey, PA : Information Science Reference.

Asimov, I. (1977). *I, robot* (1st ed.). New York: Ballantine Books.

Bailenson, J., & Blascovich, J. (2011). Infinite Reality: Avatars, Eternal Life, New Worlds, and the Dawn of the Virtual Revolution. HarperCollins e-books.

Bailenson, J., & Gurley, G. (2013). Infinite Reality.

Bailey, D. (2014). *Hyperreality: The merging of the physical and digital worlds* (Masters). University of Brighton.

Bainbridge, W. (2010). *The Warcraft civilization* (1st ed.). Cambridge, Ma.: MIT Press.

Banbury, A., Roots, A., & Nancarrow, S. (2014). Rapid review of applications of e-health and remote monitoring for rural residents. *Australian Journal Of Rural Health*, 22(5), 211-222. http://dx.doi.org/10.1111/ajr.12127

Bashir, I. (2017). *Mastering Blockchain (1)* (1st ed.). Packt Publishing.

Baudrillard, J. (1981). *Simulacra and simulation*. Originally published in French by Editions Galilee: Editions Galilee translated into English onto PDF.

Bergson, H., Jacobson, L., & Dingle, H. (1965). *Duration and simultaneity*. Indianapolis: Bobbs-Merrill.

Berke, A. (2017). How Safe Are Blockchains? It Depends. *Harvard Business Review*, 1-6.

Bertrand, P., Gonzalez-Franco, D., Cherene, C., & Pointeau, A. 'The Machine to Be Another': embodiment performance to promote empathy among individuals.

Best Branded Google VR Cardboards. (2017). *Best Branded Google VR Cardboards*. https://www.viarbox.com/single-post/2017/01/20/Virtual-Reality-HMDs-2016-Sales-Numbers

Be there, together.. AltspaceVR Inc. Retrieved 17 April 2017, from https://altvr.com/

Bishop, J. (2015). *Psychological and social implications surrounding internet and gaming addiction* (1st ed.). Hershey, PA : Information Science Reference.

Blascovich, J., & Bailenson, J. (2011). *Infinite reality*. New York: William Morrow.

Blockchain Based Anti-Counterfeit Solution. (2017). *Blockverify.io*. Retrieved 11 April 2017, from http://www.blockverify.io/

Blockchain solutions for Automotive. (2017). *Reply.com*. Retrieved 11 April 2017, from http://www.reply.com/en/content/thats-mine

Boellstorff, T. (2015). *Coming of age in Second Life* (1st ed.).

Botterbusch, H., & Talab, R. (2009). Ethical Issues in Second Life. *Techtrends*, *53*(1), 9-13. http://dx.doi.org/10.1007/s11528-009-0227-4

Bowyer, K. & Burge, M. (2013). *Handbook of Iris Recognition* (1st ed.). London: Springer London.

Brewster, S. (2017). *Despite their hyped debut, virtual-reality headsets had sluggish sales in 2016. MIT Technology Review.* https://www.technologyreview.com/s/603208/behind-the-numbers-of-virtual-realitys-sluggish-debut/*Breakroom.* (2017). *We make breakroom.* Retrieved 10 March 2017, from http://murevr.com/#about

Butt, A., & Stanacevic, M. (2014). Implementation of Mind Control Robot. *IEEE Long Island Systems, Applications And Technology (LISAT) Conference 2014.* http://dx.doi.org/10.1109/lisat.2014.6845218

Cameron, J. (2009). *Avatar. IMDb.* Retrieved 18 April 2017, from http://www.imdb.com/title/tt0499549/

Cassell, W. (2015). *An Overview of Businesses Owned by Microsoft (MSFT). Investopedia.* from http://www.investopedia.com/articles/investing/120715/overview-businesses-owned-microsoft.asp

Castronova, E., Knowles, I., & Ross, T. (2015). Policy questions raised by virtual economies. *Telecommunications Policy, 39*(9), 787-795. http://dx.doi.org/10.1016/j.telpol.2014.12.002

Chan, M. (2014). *Virtual Reality: Representations in Contemporary Media* (1st ed.). New York: Bloomsbury Academic USA.

Chuang, Y. (2006). Massively Multiplayer Online Role-Playing Game-Induced Seizures:

ANeglected Health Problem in Internet Addiction. *Cyberpsychology & Behavior*, *9*(4), 451-456. http://dx.doi.org/10.1089/cpb.2006.9.451

Ciaian, P., Rajcaniova, M., & Kancs, d. (2016). The digital agenda of virtual currencies: Can BitCoin become a global currency?. *Information Systems And E-Business Management*, *14*(4), 883-919. http://dx.doi.org/10.1007/s10257-016-0304-0

Cline, E. (2011). *Ready Player One*. New York: Crown Publishers.

Coker, T., Elliott, M., Schwebel, D., Windle, M., Toomey, S., & Tortolero, S. et al. (2015). Media Violence Exposure and Physical Aggression in Fifth-Grade Children. *Academic Pediatrics*, *15*(1), 82-88. http://dx.doi.org/10.1016/j.acap.2014.09.008

Crypto-Currency Market Capitalizations. (2017). *Coinmarketcap.com*. Retrieved 29 January 2017, from https://coinmarketcap.com/

Daugman, J. (2004). How Iris Recognition Works. *IEEE Transactions On Circuits And Systems For Video Technology*, *14*(1), 21-30. doi:10.1109/tcsvt.2003.818350

Del Pozo, I., & Iturralde, M. (2015). CI: A New Encryption Mechanism for Instant Messaging in Mobile Devices. *Procedia Computer Science*, *63*, 533-538. http://dx.doi.org/10.1016/j.procs.2015.08.381

Dibrova, A. (2016). Virtual Currency: New Step in Monetary Development. *Procedia - Social And*

Behavioral Sciences, 229, 42-49.
http://dx.doi.org/10.1016/j.sbspro.2016.07.112

Drescher, D. (2017). *Blockchain basics* (1st ed.). Apress.

Drew, J. (2013). How to open new doors by closing your office. *Journal Of Accountancy*, 24-29.

Dwyer, G. (2015). The economics of Bitcoin and similar private digital currencies. *Journal Of Financial Stability*, *17*, 81-91. http://dx.doi.org/10.1016/j.jfs.2014.11.006

Dubberley, S., Griffin, E., & Mert Bal, H. *Making Secondary Trauma a Primary Issue: A Study of Eyewitness Media and Vicarious Trauma on the Digital Frontline. Eyewitnessmediahub.com*. from http://eyewitnessmediahub.com/research/vicarious-trauma

Ensslin, A., & Muse, E. (2011). *Creating second lives* (1st ed.). New York: Routledge.

Estupinan, S., Rebelo, F., Noriega, P., Ferreira, C., & Duarte, E. (2013). Can Virtual Reality Increase Emotional Responses (Arousal and Valence)? A Pilot Study. *Lecture Notes In Computer Science 8518:541-549 · January 2013*.

European Banking Authority. (2014). *EBA Opinion on 'virtual currencies'*. EBA.

Eye tracking in VR headsets is the future, and it's starting now. (2016). *CNET*. https://www.cnet.com/news/eye-tracking-vr-headsets-future-mwc-virtual-reality-oculus-samsung-gear/

Ewalt, D. (2016). Disruption Machine. *Forbes*, 76-86.

Fairfield, J. (2012). MIXED REALITY: HOW THE LAWS OF VIRTUAL WORLDS GOVERN EVERYDAY LIFE. *BERKELEY TECHNOLOGY LAW JOURNAL, 27*(55), 54-84.

Feltham, J. (2016). *Steam has 107 VR games on sale — and here are the 6 best. VentureBeat.* Retrieved 17 April 2017, from https://venturebeat.com/2016/06/25/steam-has-107-vr-games-on-sale-and-here-are-the-6-best/

Ferguson, C. & Beresin, E. (2017). Social science's curious war with pop culture and how it was lost: The media violence debate and the risks it holds for social science. *Preventive Medicine, 99,* 69-76. http://dx.doi.org/10.1016/j.ypmed.2017.02.009

Fico, P. (2016). Virtual Currencies and Blockchains Potential Impacts on Financial Market Infrastructures and on Corporate Ownership. *SSRN Electronic Journal.* http://dx.doi.org/10.2139/ssrn.2736035

Florez, Z., Logreira, R., Munoz, M., & Vargas, J. (2016). Architecture of instant messaging systems for secure data transmision. *2016 IEEE International Carnahan Conference On Security Technology (ICCST).* http://dx.doi.org/10.1109/ccst.2016.7815685

Fogel, J. (2011). INSTANT MESSAGING COMMUNICATION: SELF- DISCLOSURE, Del Pozo, I., & Iturralde, M. (2015). CI: A New Encryption Mechanism for Instant Messaging in Mobile Devices. *Procedia Computer Science,*

63, 533-538.
http://dx.doi.org/10.1016/j.procs.2015.08.381

Forster, E. M. (n.d.). *The Machine Stops*. First published in the Oxford and Cambridge Review, November 1909.

Fox-Brewster, T. (2015). *Forbes Welcome. Forbes.com.* http://www.forbes.com/sites/thomasbrewster /2015/03/05/clone-putins-eyes-using-google-images/#352621984f85

Fox, J., Bailenson, J., & Tricase, L. (2013). The embodiment of sexualized virtual selves: The Proteus effect and experiences of self-objectification via avatars. *Computers In Human Behavior, 29*(3), 930-938. http://dx.doi.org/10.1016/j.chb.2012.12.027

Frank, A. (2016). *I Worked in a VR Office, and It Was Actually Awesome - Motherboard. Motherboard.* Retrieved 10 March 2017, from https://motherboard.vice.com/en_us/article/i -worked-in-a-vr-office-and-it-was-actually-awesome

Galbally, J. & Gomez-Barrero, M. (2016). A review of iris anti-spoofing. *2016 4Th International Conference On Biometrics And Forensics (IWBF)*. doi:10.1109/iwbf.2016.7449676

Gelernter, D. (1992). *Mirror worlds or the day software puts of the universe in a shoebox* (1st ed.). New York: Oxford University Press.

Google Earth VR. (2017). *Vr.google.com.* from https://vr.google.com/earth/

Google Timeline. (2017). *Datesandevents.org.* from http://www.datesandevents.org/events-timelines/18-google-timeline.htm

Grevstad, E. (2016). All signs point to telecommuting. *PC Magazine.*

Hansen, M. (2006). *New philosophy for new media* (1st ed.). Cambridge, Mass.: MIT.

Hawryluk, G., & Guan, J. (2016). Advancements in the mind-machine interface: towards re-establishment of direct cortical control of limb movement in spinal cord injury. *Neural Regeneration Research, 11*(7), 1060. http://dx.doi.org/10.4103/1673-5374.187026

Hayworth, K. (2012). ELECTRON IMAGING TECHNOLOGY FOR WHOLE BRAIN NEURAL CIRCUIT MAPPING. *International Journal Of Machine Consciousness, 04*(01), 87-108. http://dx.doi.org/10.1142/s1793843012400057

Hayworth, K. (2016). *Mind Uploading.* Skeptic, p. 15.

He, D., Habermeier, K., Leckow, R., Haksar, V., Almeida, Y., Kashima, M., ... Verdugo-Yepes, C. (2016). Virtual Currencies and Beyond: Initial Considerations. INTERNATIONAL MONETARY FUND. Retrieved from https://www.imf.org/external/pubs/ft/sdn/2016/sdn1603.pdf

Hering, C. (2017). *ECHO - Free Encrypted Private Chat + Instant Cloud Money Transfer. ECHO APP.* Retrieved 10 April 2017, from https://my-echo.com/

Higgins, S., & Southurst, J. (2016). *DARPA Seeks Blockchain Messaging System for Battlefield Use - CoinDesk. CoinDesk.* from http://www.coindesk.com/darpa-seeks-blockchain-messaging-system-for-battlefield-back-office-use/

Hill, E., Miller, B., Weiner, S., & Colihan, J. (1998). INFLUENCES OF THE VIRTUAL OFFICE ON ASPECTS OF WORK AND WORK/LIFE BALANCE. *Personnel Psychology, 51*(3), 667-683. http://dx.doi.org/10.1111/j.1744-6570.1998.tb00256.x

Hill, E., Ferris, M., & Märtinson, V. (2003). Does it matter where you work? A comparison of how three work venues (traditional office, virtual office, and home office) influence aspects of work and personal/family life. *Journal Of Vocational Behavior, 63*(2), 220-241. http://dx.doi.org/10.1016/s0001-8791(03)00042-3

History & Evolution Of Microsoft Office Software. (2016). *The Windows Club.* from http://www.thewindowsclub.com/history-evolution-microsoft-office-software

Home - FOVE Eye Tracking Virtual Reality Headset. (2017). *FOVE Eye Tracking Virtual Reality Headset.* https://www.getfove.com/

Hoser, T. (2016). Blockchain basics, commercial impacts and governance challenges. *Governance Directions,* (Vol 68 Issue 10), 608-612.

How phone Iris Scanners Work. (2016). *The Press,* A14.

Huberty, M. (2015). Can we vote with our tweet? On the perennial difficulty of election forecasting with social media. *International Journal Of Forecasting, 31*(3), 992-1007. http://dx.doi.org/10.1016/j.ijforecast.2014.08.005

Iansiti, M. & Lakhani, K. (2017). The Truth about Blockchain. *Harvard Business Review*.

Imel, D. (2017). *The best multiplayer VR games. VR Source*. Retrieved 17 April 2017, from http://vrsource.com/best-multiplayer-vr-games-8810/

INTIMACY, AND DISINHIBITION. *Journal Of Communications Research, 2*(1), 13-19.

Jagneux, D. (2016). *'LightVR' Wants You To Create Your Own Virtual Office Space. UploadVR*. Retrieved 10 March 2017, from https://uploadvr.com/lightvr-personalized-virtual-office-space-desktop/

Jeong, E., Kim, D., Lee, D., & Lee, H. (2016). A Study of Digital Game Addiction from Aggression, Loneliness and Depression Perspectives. *2016 49Th Hawaii International Conference On System Sciences (HICSS)*. http://dx.doi.org/10.1109/hicss.2016.470

Kassan, P. (2016). *Uploading your mind does not compute*. Skeptic, p. 22.

Khorakhun, C., & Bhatti, S. (2014). Using Online Social Media Platforms for Ubiquitous, Personal Health Monitoring. In *2014 IEEE 16th International Conference on e-Health Networking, Applications and Services (Healthcom* (pp. 287-292).

Kroeger, F. (2015). The development, escalation and collapse of system trust: From the financial crisis to society at large. *European Management Journal, 33*(6), 431-437. http://dx.doi.org/10.1016/j.emj.2015.08.001

Kubát, M. (2015). Virtual Currency Bitcoin in the Scope of Money Definition and Store of Value. *Procedia Economics And Finance, 30*, 409-416. http://dx.doi.org/10.1016/s2212-5671(15)01308-8

Lackner, J., & DiZio, P. (2014). Virtual environments and the cyberadaptaion syndrome.

Lamkin, P. (2017). *PlayStation VR Sales Near 1 Million With Huge VR Boom Predicted. Forbes.com.*, from https://www.forbes.com/sites/paullamkin/2017/02/27/playstation-vr-sales-near-1-million-with-huge-vr-boom-predicted/#1d39cbd79e6c

Leavitt, N. (2005). Instant messaging: a new target for hackers. *Computer, 38*(7), 20-23. http://dx.doi.org/10.1109/mc.2005.234

Lecher, C. (2015). *The FBI has collected 430,000 iris scans in a so-called 'pilot program'. The Verge.* http://www.theverge.com/2016/7/12/12148044/fbi-iris-pilot-program-ngi- biometric-database-aclu-privacy-act

Lee, P. (2017). Blockchain SHIFTS from theory to practice. *Euromoney*, 72-77.

Lee, P. (2016). BANKS TAKE OVER THE BLOCKCHAIN. *Euromoney*, (Vol. 47 Issue 566), p92-99, 8p.

Lee, S., Lee, C., Kwak, D., Ha, J., Kim, J., & Zhang, B. (2017). Dual-memory neural networks for modeling cognitive activities of humans via wearable sensors. *Neural Networks.* http://dx.doi.org/10.1016/j.neunet.2017.02.008

Leibniz, G., & Strickland, L. (2014). *Leibniz's Monadology* (1st ed.). Edinburgh: Edinburgh University Press.

Leinonen, H. (2016). Virtual currencies and distributed ledger technology: What is new under the sun and what is hyped repackaging?. ' *Journal Of Payments Strategy & Systems,* *10*(2), 132-152.

Loseva, E., Lipinsky, L., & Kuklina, A. (2015). Eensembles of neural networks with application of multi-objective self-configuring genetic programming in forecasting problems. In *2015 11th International Conference on Natural Computation (ICNC) Natural Computation (ICNC.*

Lwan, K. *9 Companies acquired and owned by Facebook | FBtutorial.com. FBtutorial.com.* from http://fbtutorial.com/9-companies-acquired-and-owned-by-facebook/

Madary, M., & Metzinger, T. (2016). Recommendations for Good Scientific Practice and the Consumers of VR-Technology. *Frontiers In Robotics And AI, 3.* http://dx.doi.org/10.3389/frobt.2016.00003

Maiberg, E. (2016). *Why Is 'Second Life' Still a Thing?. Motherboard.* Retrieved 16 April 2017, from https://motherboard.vice.com/en_us/article/why-is-second-life-still-a-thing-gaming-virtual-reality

Mainelli, M. (2017). Blockchain Will Help Us Prove Our Identities in a Digital World. *Harvard Business Review.*

Malki, A., Yang, C., Wang, N., & Li, Z. (2015). Mind guided motion control of robot manipulator using EEG signals. *2015 5Th International Conference On Information Science And Technology (ICIST).* http://dx.doi.org/10.1109/icist.2015.7289033

Market Capitalization. (2017). Blockchain.info. Retrieved 29 January 2017, from https://blockchain.info/charts/market-cap

Marshall, A. (2016). *Powered by Blockchain, New Decentralized Messenger to Save Data, Battery and Time. CoinTelegraph.* from https://cointelegraph.com/news/powered-by-blockchain-new-decentralized-messenger-to-save-data-battery-and-time Martindale, J. (2016). *Compute from the beach (or Mars) with Space, a VR office environment. Digital Trends.* Retrieved 10 March 2017, from http://www.digitaltrends.com/virtual-reality/space-virtual-reality-office/

Marvin, R. (2017). BLOCKCHAIN: THE INVISIBLE TECH THAT'S CHANGING THE WORLD. *PC Magazine,* p91-113, 23p.

McCloud, S. (1994). *Understanding comics.* New York: HarperPerennial.

Messenger, J. & Gschwind, L. (2016). Three generations of Telework: New ICTs and the (R)evolution from Home Office to Virtual Office. *New Technology, Work And Employment, 31*(3), 195-208. http://dx.doi.org/10.1111/ntwe.12073

Microsoft by the Numbers. (2017). *Microsoft by the Numbers*. from https://news.microsoft.com/bythenumbers/

Monica, P. (2016). *Google is worth more than Apple again. CNNMoney.* from http://money.cnn.com/2016/05/12/investing/apple-google-alphabet-most-valuable/

Morabito, V. (2017). *Business innovation through blockchain* (1st ed.). Springer International Publishing.

Mougayar, W. & Buterin, V. (2016). *The Business Blockchain* (1st ed.). John Wiley & Sons, Incorporated, 2016.

Nakamoto, S. Bitcoin: A Peer-to-Peer Electronic Cash System.

Nazir, M. & Lui, C. (2016). A Brief History of Virtual Economy. *Journal Of Virtual Worlds Research*, 9(1).

New MMORPGs 2017: 11 new and upcoming MMOs worth looking out for. (2017). *PCGamesN.* from https://www.pcgamesn.com/new-mmos

Noor, A. (2016). The HoloLens Revolution. *Mechanical Engineering*, 30-36.

O'Brolcháin, F., Jacquemard, T., Monaghan, D., O'Connor, N., Novitzky, P., & Gordijn, B. (2015). The Convergence of Virtual Reality and Social Networks: Threats to Privacy and Autonomy. *Science And Engineering Ethics*, 22(1), 1-29. http://dx.doi.org/10.1007/s11948-014-9621-1

Ohlheiser, A. (2017). *Facebook Live wants to give people a voice, but it's mostly noticed for violence. chicagotribune.com.* from

http://www.chicagotribune.com/bluesky/tech
nology/ct-facebook-live-violence-wp-bsi-
20170108-story.html

Oostveen, A. & Dimitrova, D. (2015). *Iris scanners
can now identify us from 40 feet away. The
Conversation.*
https://theconversation.com/iris-scanners-
can-now-identify-us-from-40- feet-away-42141

Perry, T. (2017). Augmented reality: forget the glasses.
IEEE Spectrum, 54(1), 36-39.
doi:10.1109/mspec.2017.7802744

Piwek, L., & Joinson, A. (2016). "What do they
snapchat about?" Patterns of use in time-
limited instant messaging service. *Computers
In Human Behavior, 54*, 358-367.
http://dx.doi.org/10.1016/j.chb.2015.08.026

Proof of Existence. (2017). *Proofofexistence.com.*
Retrieved 11 April 2017, from
https://proofofexistence.com/about

Rattani, A. & Derakhshani, R. (2017). Ocular
biometrics in the visible spectrum: A survey.
Image And Vision Computing, 59, 1-16.
doi:10.1016/j.imavis.2016.11.019

Raymundo, O. (2016). Tim Cook: Augmented reality
will be an essential part of your daily life, like
the iPhone. *IOS Central.*

Report of the Commonwealth Working Group on
virtual currencies. (2016). *Commonwealth
Law Bulletin, 42*(2), 263-324.
http://dx.doi.org/10.1080/03050718.2016.119
5979

Ricci, A., Piunti, M., Tummolini, L., & Castelfranchi,
C. (2015). The Mirror World: Preparing for

Mixed-Reality Living. *IEEE Pervasive Computing, 14*(2), 60-63. http://dx.doi.org/10.1109/mprv.2015.44

Roberts, J. (2017). *VR Sales Numbers Are Wet Blanket on Adoption Hopes. Fortune.com.* from http://fortune.com/2017/02/19/virtual-reality-vr-sales/?iid=sr-link1

Roettgers, J. (2015). *AltspaceVR Raises $10 Million to Make Virtual Reality Social. Variety.* from http://variety.com/2015/digital/news/altspace vr-raises-10-million-to-make-virtual-reality-social-1201551949/

Rognini, G., & Blanke, O. (2016). Cognetics: Robotic Interfaces for the Conscious Mind. *Trends In Cognitive Sciences, 20*(3), 162-164. http://dx.doi.org/10.1016/j.tics.2015.12.002

Rubin, P. (2017). *Facebook's Bizarre VR App Is Exactly Why Zuck Bought Oculus. Wired.com.* https://www.wired.com/2017/04/facebook-spaces-vr-for-your-friends/

Shir, F. (2015). Mind-Reading System - A Cutting-Edge Technology. *International Journal Of Advanced Computer Science And Applications, 6*(7). http://dx.doi.org/10.14569/ijacsa.2015.06070 2

Smyth, S. (2009). Back to the Future: Crime and Punishment in Second Life. *Rutgers Computer And Technology Law Journal, 36*(1), 18-72.

Steinicke, F., & Bruder, G. (2014). A Self-Experimentation Report about Long-Term Use of Fully-Immersive Technology.

Steinicke, F. (2016). *Being Really Virtual* (1st ed.). Cham: Springer International Publishing.

Stephygraph, L., Arunkumar, N., & Venkatraman, V. (2015). Wireless Mobile Robot Control through Human Machine Interface using Brain Signals.

Stuart, S. (2017). How VR Holograms Can Train Everyone From Hairdressers to Astronauts. *PC Magazine.*

STATS | YouTube Company Statistics - Statistic Brain. (2017). *Statistic Brain.* Retrieved 12 March 2017, from http://www.statisticbrain.com/youtube-statistics/

Sullins, J. (2000). Transcending the meat: immersive technologies and computer mediated bodies. *Journal Of Experimental & Theoretical Artificial Intelligence, 12*(1), 13-22. http://dx.doi.org/10.1080/095281300146281

Suzor, N. (2010). THE ROLE OF THE RULE OF LAW IN VIRTUAL COMMUNITIES. *BERKELEY TECHNOLOGY LAW JOURNAL, 25,* 1817-1885.

Tafforin, C., Vinokhodova, A., Chekalina, A., & Gushin, V. (2015). Correlation of etho-social and psycho-social data from "Mars-500" interplanetary simulation. *Acta Astronautica, 111,* 19-28. http://dx.doi.org/10.1016/j.actaastro.2015.02.005

Tang, H., Tan, K., & Yi, Z. (2007). *Neural networks* (1st ed.). Berlin: Springer.

Terec-Vlad, L. (2015). From Divine Transcendence to the Artificial One. Challenges of the New

Technologies. *Postmodern Openings, 06*(01), 119-129. http://dx.doi.org/10.18662/po/2015.0601.08

Terec-Vlad, L. (2015). What about Eternal Life? A Transhumanist Perspective. *Postmodern Openings, 6*(2), 33-41. http://dx.doi.org/10.18662/po/2015.0602.03

The Machine to be Another. (2017). *The Machine to be Another.* from http://www.themachinetobeanother.org/

Underwood, S. (2016). Blockchain beyond bitcoin. Communications Of The ACM, *59*(11), 15-17. http://dx.doi.org/10.1145/2994581

VARMA, N., & RICCI, R. (2015). Impact of Remote Monitoring on Clinical Outcomes. *Journal Of Cardiovascular Electrophysiology, 26*(12), 1388-1395. http://dx.doi.org/10.1111/jce.12829

Vazharov, S. & Vazharov, S. (2017). *The Best 360-Degree Cameras for Capturing Your Surroundings. Best Products.* from http://www.bestproducts.com/tech/gadgets/news/g1752/360-degree-cameras/

Wachowski, L., & Wachowski, L. (1999). *The Matrix.* Retrieved from http://www.imdb.com/title/tt0133093/

Walbesser, J. (2014). FINDING MEANING IN THE DEATH OF VIRTUAL IDENTITIES. *Buffalo Intellectual Property Law Journal, 10http://www.citethisforme.com/cite/journal*, 70-91.

Warner, M. (2016). *DARPA Contract to Verify Blockchain Integrity Monitoring Awarded to Galois and Guardtime Federal | Chain-*

Finance.com. Blockchain-finance.com. from http://blockchain-finance.com/2016/09/17/darpa-contract-to-verify-blockchain-integrity-monitoring-awarded-to-galois-and-guardtime-federal/

Wen, D., Zhang, X., & Lei, J. (2017). Consumers' perceived attitudes to wearable devices in health monitoring in China: A survey study. *Computer Methods And Programs In Biomedicine, 140,* 131-137. http://dx.doi.org/10.1016/j.cmpb.2016.12.009

Wingfield, N. (2017). *Popularity of Sony's PlayStation VR Surprises Even the Company. Mobile.nytimes.com.* from https://mobile.nytimes.com/2017/02/26/business/sony-playstation-vr-sales.html?_r=0&referer=https://www.google.ca/Wood, E., Wright, J., Harris, E., Mind, T., Clavier, T., & L'Oeil, T. (2016). *Westworld (TV Series 2016–). IMDb.* from http://www.imdb.com/title/tt0475784/

Wu, T., Lu, Y., Gong, X., & Gupta, S. (2017). A study of active usage of mobile instant messaging application. *Information Development, 33*(2), 153-168. http://dx.doi.org/10.1177/0266666916646814

You can now fly around Google Earth in virtual reality. (2016). *The Verge.* from http://www.theverge.com/2016/11/16/13643550/google-earth-vr-htc-vive-release

Zheng, J. & Zhang, Q. (2016). Priming effect of computer game violence on children's aggression levels. *Social Behavior And Personality: An International Journal, 44*(10),

1747-1759.
http://dx.doi.org/10.2224/sbp.2016.44.10.174
7

ZINGALES, L. (2015). Presidential Address: Does
Finance Benefit Society?. *The Journal Of
Finance*, *70*(4), 1327-1363.
http://dx.doi.org/10.1111/jofi.12295